✐ P9-CDL-562

What People Are Saying about *Leadership and the Art of Struggle*

"A very fresh and inspiring perspective that constructively embraces the natural tensions that all leaders encounter every day. I heartily recommend it to any leader who aspires to lead and contribute more fully."
—**Douglas R. Conant, former President, CEO, and Director, Campbell Soup Company, and coauthor of the *New York Times* bestseller *TouchPoints***

"Steven courageously confronts the element of struggle, which is frequently overlooked in all the leadership hoopla. It's time we had an open and honest conversation about this integral and vital aspect of leadership."
—**Ken Melrose, former CEO, Toro**

"Steven guides you on a journey that can be deeply fulfilling as well as enlightening. I recommend this book for any leader who wants to engage more authentically and constructively in a complex and ever-changing world."
—**Mary Brainerd, CEO, HealthPartners**

"*Leadership and the Art of Struggle* contains compelling stories of great leaders who have struggled with various facets of their leadership responsibility. It offers practical advice and tools to help you deal more effectively with the inevitable struggles of leadership."
—**Trudy Rautio, President and CEO, Carlson**

"If you are leading an organization of any kind today or desire to lead one in the future, you need to read this book."
—**Frank Russomanno, former CEO, Imation**

"The must-read leadership book of the year. It is one of the most intelligent, revealing, and practical books on the subject I have ever read. It confronts a vital truth about leadership: that challenge is the crucible for greatness and that these adversities introduce us to ourselves. Buy this book immediately, read it with a sense of urgency, and apply it with the commitment of a disciple. You and those you work with will benefit greatly when you do."
—**Jim Kouzes, coauthor of the bestselling *The Leadership Challenge***

"Steven Snyder covers all the bases from channeling your energy to managing conflict, including a great segment about overcoming your leadership blind spots. Full of real-life examples of leaders who emerged from tough times better and stronger than before, this encouraging book is a must-read!"
—**Ken Blanchard, coauthor of *The One Minute Manager* and *Great Leaders Grow***

"The leadership journey is rewarding but definitely not easy. *Leadership and the Art of the Struggle* gives you clear and compelling advice on transforming pitfalls into possibilities."
—**Jodee Kozlak, Executive Vice President, Human Resources, Target**

"Snyder has opened an intriguing and insightful portal into the challenge of leadership. You'll be inspired and invigorated with ideas that you can immediately put into action."

—**Kevin Wilde, Chief Learning Officer, General Mills, and author of** *Dancing with the Talent Stars*

"Life in a start-up is chaotic, intense, and unpredictable. Snyder knows this world well and gives you sage advice on how to remain grounded, focused, and energized. This is a book that every entrepreneur or would-be entrepreneur should read."

—**Michael Gorman, Managing Director, Split Rock Partners**

"Snyder boldly tackles a subject that every leader needs to master. Sometimes leadership is a struggle, and these are the times that really put us to the test. This insightful book will teach you how to thrive during life's most challenging moments."

—**Marshall Goldsmith,** *New York Times* **bestselling author of** *Mojo* **and** *What Got You Here Won't Get You There*

"This book resonates to the core. It gives us grounding and offers precise practices for locating our work deep in the soul. Steven makes the dive into the waters of purposeful living and leading deep and attractive. What a delightful dive!"

—**Richard Leider, bestselling author of** *The Power of Purpose* **and coauthor of** *Repacking Your Bags*

"The French writer Albert Camus tells us, 'In the depth of winter, I finally learned that there was within me an invincible summer.' Snyder wisely observes that we can best strike a blow against tragedy and disappointment by using them as inspiration to make a positive difference in the lives of others through our personal leadership."

—**Marilyn Carlson Nelson, Chairman, Carlson**

"This is the right book for these times. Leadership has become more difficult in the chaotic world we live in; Steven acknowledges that and draws on his own deep experience and the lessons learned of others to help any new, aspiring, or well-worn leader!"

—**Beverly Kaye, founder of Career Systems International and coauthor of** *Love 'Em or Lose 'Em* **and** *Help Them Grow or Watch Them Go*

"*Leadership and the Art of Struggle* deserves to be a leadership classic! Snyder brilliantly charts a course to strengthen ourselves through the important crucibles of challenge and adversity. If you want to build more authentic leadership in yourself and others, get this life-changing book!"

—**Kevin Cashman, Senior Partner, Korn/Ferry International, and bestselling author of** *The Pause Principle* **and** *Leadership from the Inside Out*

Leadership
and the
Art *of* Struggle

Leadership

and the

Art *of* Struggle

How Great Leaders Grow through
Challenge and Adversity

Steven Snyder

Berrett–Koehler Publishers, Inc.
a BK Business book

The information in this book is based on the research of Steven Snyder and publicly available material. A few names and details have been changed to protect the identities of those involved. These are indicated in the notes.

Berrett-Koehler Publishers, Inc.
1333 Broadway, Suite 1000, Oakland, CA 94612-1921
Tel: (510) 817-2277   Fax: (510) 817-2278   www.bkconnection.com

Ordering Information

Quantity sales. Special discounts are available on quantity purchases by corporations, associations, and others. For details, contact the "Special Sales Department" at the Berrett-Koehler address above.

Individual sales. Berrett-Koehler publications are available through most bookstores. They can also be ordered directly from Berrett-Koehler:
Tel: (800) 929-2929; Fax: (802) 864-7626; www.bkconnection.com.

Orders for college textbook/course adoption use. Please contact Berrett-Koehler:
Tel: (800) 929-2929; Fax: (802) 864-7626.

Orders by U.S. trade bookstores and wholesalers. Please contact Ingram Publisher Services, Tel: (800) 509-4887; Fax: (800) 838-1149; E-mail: customer.service@ ingrampublisherservices.com; or visit www.ingrampublisherservices.com/Ordering for details about electronic ordering.

Berrett-Koehler and the BK logo are registered trademarks of Berrett-Koehler Publishers, Inc.

Printed in Canada

Berrett-Koehler books are printed on long-lasting acid-free paper. When it is available, we choose paper that has been manufactured by environmentally responsible processes. These may include using trees grown in sustainable forests, incorporating recycled paper, minimizing chlorine in bleaching, or recycling the energy produced at the paper mill.

Library of Congress Cataloging-in-Publication Data
Snyder, Steven, 1954-
    Leadership and the art of struggle : how great leaders grow through challenge and adversity / Steven Snyder.
        p. cm.
    Includes bibliographical references and index.
    ISBN 978-1-60994-644-9 (pbk.)
1. Leadership. 2. Success in business. I. Title.
    HD57.7.S6922 2013
    658.4'092—dc23

                                                                    2012043676

21   20   19   18   17   16   10   9   8   7   6   5   4   3   2

Cover design by Ian Shimkoviak/The Book Designers.
Interior design and composition by Gary Palmatier, Ideas to Images.
Elizabeth von Radics, copyeditor; Mike Mollett, proofreader; Medea Minnich, indexer.

To Sherry Stern, my loving wife of 34 years,
who saw this book within me even before I did
and encouraged me to write it

Contents

Foreword

by Bill George

*D*O YOUR STRUGGLES MAKE YOU A BETTER LEADER? IS IT NECESSARY to overcome severe challenges to become an outstanding leader?

Yes, says Steven Snyder emphatically in this remarkable book. "Clearly, struggle and leadership are intertwined," he writes. "Great leaders use failure as a wake-up call."

That's a conclusion many would-be leaders are reluctant to accept. In today's world, society often searches for perfect leaders. When their actions reveal their weaknesses and shortcomings, the general public turns away from them and continues the impossible search for perfection. Media pundits, eager to condemn our leaders, pile on the criticism. Like the two tramps in Samuel Beckett's *Waiting for Godot,* who are hoping for the savior to lead them out of their misery, the public is still searching for the perfect leader. Instead of stepping up to leadership themselves, many people continue to drift through life and fail to realize their full potential as human beings and as leaders.

In *Leadership and the Art of Struggle,* Snyder takes an entirely different tack. He believes, as I do, that failure is a great teacher. To learn from it, you must be prepared to face its painful realities. That's what Steve Jobs did after being ousted from the company he founded. Had he not been forced to face his own shortcomings, he never could have returned to create the success that led Apple to become the most highly valued company of all time. The same is true of Oprah Winfrey, who had to face the pain of the sexual abuse she endured as a young girl. When she did so, she changed her message to empowering people and became the most successful media personality of her era.

In a room filled with 125 powerful large-company chief executive officers, I once asked Jamie Dimon, JPMorgan's chair and CEO, what his defining experience was. Rather than citing his great success at JPMorgan, he replied instantly, "I got fired . . . by my mentor of 22 years." Learning from that experience, Dimon bounced back and became the world's leading financial services CEO. Forced to face the reality of his bank's $6 billion in trading losses, he took immediate responsibility for them. He went on *Meet the Press* and said, "We made a terrible, egregious mistake. We were stupid. There's almost no excuse for it."

The realities that Snyder addresses represent a fundamental building block required to develop healthy, effective leaders who are committed to building a society devoted to the well-being of all. Only in acknowledging our own flaws and vulnerabilities can we become authentic leaders who empower people to perform to the best of their abilities.

Shortly after joining the Harvard Business School (HBS) faculty in 2004, I initiated a research project to determine the characteristics of authentic leaders and the ways they developed their leadership. My HBS colleagues encouraged me to discover the traits, characteristics, and styles of these successful leaders. Then my HBS research associate presented me with discouraging news: 1,400 previous studies had been unsuccessful in determining these definitive characteristics, as all failed to establish statistical validity or replicability. Nevertheless we went ahead with our project. Two skilled researchers and I interviewed 125 leaders ages 23 to 93, generating 3,000 pages of transcripts. To our disappointment nothing definitive emerged about the leaders' characteristics. Rather many leaders said, "Let me just talk about what's important to me."

In reviewing the transcripts with our research team, I had a sickening feeling that the inputs might just turn out to be mush. But when we reread the deeply honest and personal stories these leaders told us about themselves, the conclusions jumped off the pages. It was the life stories of these leaders that shaped their leadership. Their challenging times and crucibles stoked their passion to make a difference through leading. Some of their failures—and nearly all had experienced setbacks or great hardships—had resulted from abandoning their roots and not staying grounded in who they were. We labeled these periods as "losing their way." Others faced challenges not of their own making, which nonetheless were life changing. Those who went on to greater success as leaders maintained fidelity to their life stories and who they were—their True North.

When we published these results in my 2007 book *True North*, they had great resonance with business and nonprofit leaders—from younger managers and middle managers to senior executives. I was especially surprised that the ideas struck a vital chord with very powerful CEOs, as they were so much at variance with what was being written and taught at the time.

Snyder's book takes these same themes to a much deeper and richer level, as he pushes the limits much farther than I did. He asserts that struggle is an "art to be mastered," an intrinsic aspect of leadership and an opportunity for leaders to realize their potential. That runs directly contrary to the macho image cultivated by many powerful leaders who deny their weaknesses and vulnerabilities. With that denial, they rob themselves of opportunities for deep introspection and a clearer understanding of themselves. Small wonder that many high-level leaders feel like imposters. One Stanford professor has discovered that the number one fear of top leaders is "being found out." Thus it is not surprising that many leaders fail, most often because they cannot face reality and they deny they are at risk of causing their own failures.

Snyder takes these fundamental truths of human nature and converts them into a set of well-conceived strategies and practices that enable leaders to become *grounded*—a term I was too timid to use in

True North because it sounded *soft*. Of course the real work of leaders who are getting grounded in their authenticity, their humanity, and their weaknesses and vulnerabilities, as well as their strengths, is exceptionally *hard* work.

On a personal level, it took me many years to acknowledge openly my shortcomings, weaknesses, and vulnerabilities. For that reason I wound up withholding "the real me" from colleagues at work, coming across as superconfident, aggressive, and completely focused on business results. When I began sharing my weaknesses—being impatient, lacking tact, and often coming across as intimidating—as well as the failures and the difficulties I had experienced in my lifetime, I learned that people opened up about themselves and resonated more with my leadership. I accepted that I wasn't expected to have all the answers and could more frequently admit, "I don't know." In being willing to be vulnerable, I found I could acknowledge the fears of being rejected as a leader that went back to high school and college, when I lost seven consecutive elections because others didn't want to work with me.

For many years I tried to deny my weaknesses and blame them on my father, as if I inherited them from him. It didn't work. When I finally acknowledged that these were *my* weaknesses, not his, and this was who I was, I felt the burden lifting from me. Only then could I feel comfortable in being myself. These shortcomings are still part of me, but they are far less prominent and they no longer own me as they once did. As a result, my relationships with colleagues, family members, and friends have steadily improved.

In understanding how much more people were willing to trust me after that, I recognized that "vulnerability is power," a favorite saying of author John Hope Bryant in *Love Leadership: The New Way to Lead in a Fear-Based World*. The paradox is that by acknowledging your vulnerabilities, you retain the power because others are unable to take advantage of you when you try to cover up your shortcomings and fears. At the same time, you empower others to become more authentic by acknowledging their vulnerabilities.

In teaching these ideas to senior executives, I often get puzzled looks because they have steeled themselves *not* to reveal their vulnerabilities out of fear that others might take advantage of them. Of course, the truth is precisely the opposite. In refusing to acknowledge their roles in contributing to the problems around them, many leaders repeat their mistakes rather than learn from them. They may move to another job without ever facing themselves, thinking a fresh start will obviate their difficulties.

As mindfulness expert Jon Kabat-Zinn writes, "Wherever you go, there you are." In other words, we can change the venue, but our shortcomings are with us until we acknowledge them to ourselves as well as to others. When we do so, our weaknesses steadily diminish and our strengths become more powerful. That's also the message of the positive psychology movement initiated by Martin Seligman, which is often falsely construed as burying your past difficulties rather than growing from them.

In this book Snyder provides specific strategies to deal with these issues. He pairs his strategies with a series of techniques and exercises that enable us to stay grounded and explore new pathways to grow from our experiences. In the end he shows us how to develop the adaptive energy required to prepare for the greater challenges we will face in leadership. Through this rigorous process, we can develop the focus and the discipline to work through our issues and, ultimately, to celebrate what really matters in our lives.

Having worked with many leaders who are earnestly embarking on the journey that Snyder takes us on, my advice is to not expect instant results. Being authentically self-aware and mindful of your feelings, emotions, and reactions can take many years of hard work as you peel back the layers of that unique person you are. It often takes that much time to learn how to grasp the power you have within you to be the very best you can be.

This journey can be difficult if not impossible to take on your own. We all need a team of fellow pilgrims to help us as we in turn help them along their paths. As the famous Hindu philosopher Jiddu Krishnamurti wrote, "Relationship is the mirror through which we see ourselves as we really are." With how many people do you have truly open and enduring relationships? How many of them are willing to hold a mirror up to you?

We need a support team that helps us through the most challenging times of our lives. My team starts with my wife, Penny, my faithful companion of 43 years, who has helped an engineer learn about psychology, human nature, and, most importantly, *myself.* I have also learned a great deal from the wisdom of our two sons, Jeff and Jon; my close friends; and my colleagues at Harvard Business School.

Other than Penny, nothing has been more constant and helpful than my two True North Groups—my men's group that has met weekly for 39 years and our couple's group that has met monthly for 30 years and traveled the world together. We have learned from our personal and professional challenges and helped each other along the way, through good times and especially in difficult times. Do you have a True North Group taking this exciting journey with you?

Leadership and the Art of Struggle provides you with the opportunity to learn from Steven Snyder's remarkable wisdom and the experiences of his interviewees. It is also a living guide that you can return to time after time when new situations arise. You may want to undertake this journey with your support team. That will give you the opportunity to share in one another's struggles and gain the authenticity and the mastery that characterizes wise leaders.

By going through this process, you will feel more alive, energized, and resilient than you ever believed was possible. You will become a better, more authentic leader; your relationships will become stronger and richer; and you will be able to accomplish more.

What more could you ask for in life?

Introduction

$\mathcal{I}$ WAS SPELLBOUND WATCHING THE FIRST PUBLIC DEMONSTRATION of the Lisa, Apple's first computer with a graphical user interface (GUI). Steve Jobs had introduced the Lisa to journalists in New York City the week before, and his presentations had been electrifying. The event I attended in January 1983, which took place at the old New England Life Hall, was hosted by the Boston Computer Society, the world's largest computer user group. Like many in the audience, I had been eagerly anticipating the arrival of this bold new technology that promised to bring us to the cusp of a new age of computing.

What I did not know then was that, behind his charisma and bravado, Jobs was deeply conflicted and struggling on multiple levels. He had been thrown off the Lisa team because of detrimental, counterproductive behavior. Even as he was publicly extolling the virtues of the Lisa, he was doing everything he could within Apple to undermine its success in favor of the Macintosh. Adding to the irony on a personal level, the Lisa had been named for the daughter whom Jobs had abandoned, just as he himself had been abandoned by his own parents as an infant. In May 1985, Jobs's aggressive, disrespectful, take-no-prisoners management style would contribute to his losing a power struggle with John Sculley—the chief executive officer that he had handpicked, wooed, and once called friend. Disillusioned and despondent, he left the company he had helped to found.

The Steve Jobs who emerged two decades later to deliver the 2005 Stanford University commencement address was a very different person. He had confronted his struggles, personal and professional, and had navigated through a number of challenges. He was on his way to becoming one of the most influential leaders of our time. Even though he died tragically young in 2011, his life is a testament to personal growth, leadership development, and human potential. Not only did Jobs push the boundaries of what was considered possible, he radically changed our thinking about leadership and innovation. He maximized his own contribution, left us wondering what more might have followed, and inspired us to see the benefits of shifting our perspective and thinking in new ways. Through his struggles Jobs had redefined his purpose in life and transformed his leadership energies in service to this core purpose.

Steve Jobs was not a perfect man or a perfect leader. He was a leader who struggled, like all of us, and whose life and leadership illustrated the developmental metamorphosis that is available to us all. All we need to do is choose it.

Viewing Struggle as an Art

Leadership is often a struggle. Yet societal taboos often prevent leaders from talking openly and honestly about their struggles for fear of being perceived as ineffective and inadequate. Social mores reinforce the myth that leaders are supposed to be perfect and that struggle is a sign of weakness and a source of shame. It is hard to keep these societal views in perspective, especially when facing significant challenges. This cultural programming, learned over many years, becomes ingrained, causing some leaders to lose their confidence and doubt their abilities, thinking something is wrong with them.

The best leaders learn to sidestep these unrealistic expectations by accepting themselves for who they are today while continually

striving to be better tomorrow. These individuals come to understand that struggle is a natural part of leadership and that it is often
the struggle itself that unlocks the potential for the greatest growth.
Instead of denying the struggle or feeling diminished by it, they learn
to embrace it as an art to be mastered. Consequently, they develop
skills, capabilities, and practices that help them cope with—and even
thrive in the midst of—challenge and adversity.

Everyone is at their own unique stage in the leadership contin-
uum and in their mastery of the art of struggle. Some leaders, especially those who are just starting out, may not be aware that their
behavior is counterproductive. They have no self-regulatory mechanism, no brakes. Some are so oblivious that they just plunge ahead
until they run into a brick wall. They have no awareness of how their
own choices and blind spots get them into trouble, and they blame
others for their misfortune.

Some continue to repeat the same mistakes over and over. They
go from one job to another, acting out the same patterns, reenacting
the same scripts. As these scripts play out, they produce the same predictable, unsatisfactory results. Yet they lack the insight to connect the
dots between their own unenlightened behavior and the unfavorable
outcomes they grumble about.

Great leaders use failure as a wake-up call. Instead of blaming
others, they seek out the counsel of a mentor and/or turn their attention inward for reflection and introspection. They become aware of
how their own behaviors and practices contribute to undesirable
outcomes and resolve to break from past habits, to begin anew. The
next time they encounter the same constellation of circumstances,
they try a different approach. Choosing a new script frees them from
the prison of stale thinking and unproductive behavior and leads to
an understanding of how they can work with others to achieve some
larger purpose or mission.

As these awakened individuals advance on their leadership journey, they gradually view themselves and their role as leaders in fundamentally different ways than they did earlier in their careers. They reach a place where they view leadership as an enriching, deeply human experience. They derive happiness and fulfillment from not only their successes but also the intrinsic nature of the journey itself.

My goal is to meet you where you are right now and guide you to take your leadership to the next level. If you find yourself feeling overwhelmed or intimidated at any point in the process, I urge you to press forward. I truly believe that you will come to look forward to the challenges that await you, with anticipation, eagerness, and a newfound sense of confidence. Whether you feel self-conscious or self-assured, you will learn about potential pitfalls in the road ahead and how best to avoid them.

If you are immersed in a difficult leadership challenge and feeling trapped in a situation that seems beyond your control, the ideas and the exercises in this book can help reignite your sense of empowerment and spur you to brainstorm creative new solutions. Even if you consider yourself an accomplished leader with an extensive résumé of achievements, the insights you glean from these pages may expand your view of leadership and better equip you to coach others through their own struggles.

Ultimately, I am confident that you will find value in this book because it is a synthesis of collective wisdom from extraordinary leaders. They have gone through the same struggles you have. They have found the paths that are best for them. I am certain that you will find the path that is best for you.

Fulfilling your potential as a leader requires that you think differently about leadership. You must recast your struggles as positive learning experiences and view them as necessary steps in your development as a leader. You must look at leadership through an entirely different lens.

Leadership through a Different Lens

Some years ago I heard a former classmate of mine, Joe Badaracco, speak about a course he was teaching at Harvard Business School. He and his students studied leadership through the lens of literature. Instead of the usual case studies, the course examined the lives of fictional characters in literary works such as Arthur Miller's *Death of a Salesman,* Robert Bolt's *A Man for All Seasons,* Joseph Conrad's *The Secret Sharer,* and Chinua Achebe's *Things Fall Apart.* Badaracco's premise was that fiction opens a new portal on leadership, deepening the understanding of leadership as a *human* endeavor, a reality that is often absent in other leadership approaches.

By delving into the raw humanity of these flawed yet often heroic characters, Badaracco guided his students to a compelling insight:

> *Leadership is a struggle by flawed human beings to make some important human values real and effective in the world as it is.*

This concept may push some people out of their comfort zone. In a world influenced by relentlessly upbeat urgings, leaders may feel awkward about acknowledging that they struggle. It is understandable that leaders may be too deeply embarrassed to reveal their flaws—or to admit that they even have flaws. This reluctance is why Badaracco's lens—let's call it the *Struggle Lens*—is so crucial. It offers a visceral understanding of the human condition, which is the key to unlocking leadership potential and awakening the mind to an expanded menu of choices and possibilities. Let's examine this Struggle Lens point by point.

■ *Leadership . . .* The Struggle Lens begins with several different assumptions about leadership. While other leadership models implicitly draw a distinction between leaders and followers, this lens is egalitarian: *Everyone* who engages in the struggle to make important human values real and effective is practicing leadership. Similarly, while other leadership models focus only on external behaviors, the Struggle Lens expands this view to also embrace the inner experience of the leader.

- **... is a struggle ...** Yes, leadership is a struggle, at least some of the time. It is vitally important to face this struggle head on—not hiding from it or feeling shame—because struggle is the gateway to learning and growth.

- **... by flawed human beings ...** All human beings have their own unique frailties. Some may argue that people should concentrate on developing their strengths and take no notice of their weaknesses. But conveniently ignoring blind spots, as noted in chapter 7, can lead to serious trouble. By acknowledging that you are imperfect, you give voice to a fundamental truth about what it is to be human, opening pathways for compassion, forgiveness, and healing.

- **... to make some important human values real and effective ...** Traditional leadership models emphasize the importance, and rightly so, of goal attainment. Yet an obsessive preoccupation with goals may blind a leader to circumstances in which goals and values, whether personal or organizational, are not in sync. This misalignment needs to be brought front and center so that explicit conversations can take place. What's more, not all important human values can be made real and effective in every situation, so choices must be made. What does that process look like?

- **... in the world as it is.** Leadership occurs not in some ideal world but in the real world, filled with complexity, chaos, and uncertainty. Taking action always produces consequences that ripple out into the world at large. And no matter how creative the solution, there are always limits to an individual's power and influence; some factors are simply beyond one's control. Conviction must be tempered with pragmatism.

The Struggle Lens presents a new portrait of leadership, affirming that struggle has been central to humanity throughout the ages. A new narrative surfaces, emphasizing the realization of human potential through the crucible of adversity.

While traditional leadership narratives contemplate *what* and *how*, this struggle-centric narrative probes deeper, uncovering *why*. Ultimately, it becomes clear that the actualization of important human values is at the core of all human striving.

Indeed struggle and leadership are unquestionably intertwined. A new perspective dawns when struggle is recognized as an intrinsic aspect of leadership and an opportunity for leaders to realize their full potential. When struggle is viewed as an art to be mastered, a new set of strategies and practices emerges, enabling leaders to elevate their skills to ever-greater heights.

The Art of Struggle: Mastery Practices

Although the Struggle Lens was initially focused on fictional characters, its power can be fully leveraged by using it to probe real stories of actual leaders. To that end I asked numerous corporate, nonprofit, and government leaders to recall and describe a time of great struggle in their professional careers. Rather than predefine for them what struggle was, I allowed their unique narratives to guide my inquiry.

From 151 struggle examples covering a variety of challenging situations, a distinct pattern emerged. I saw that three fundamental conditions, or defining elements, were at the heart of every episode:

- Change plays a prominent role in leadership struggle.

- This change creates a natural set of tensions.

- The tensions throw the leader off balance.

Many of these real-world struggle stories turned out well. Some did not. Outcomes were influenced largely by how effectively leaders channeled their energies to accept and embrace change and adaptively engage in the struggle. Even in the stories that ended badly, there was much learning to be gained; failures often proved to be catalysts for future growth.

How can leaders learn to adaptively and effectively channel their energies? My research reveals a set of core practices that form the backbone of this book, which is organized into three parts.

Part I, which encompasses the first five chapters, focuses on *becoming grounded*—gaining a mooring on struggle and restoring balance. After a closer look at the defining elements of struggle (change, tensions, and being out of balance), the spotlight is trained on different scripts that commonly play out as struggle unfolds. You will also be introduced to the grounding practices:

- Adopt a growth mind-set.

- Become resilient in the face of failure.

- Draw your tension map.

- Center your mind, body, and spirit.

- Find the support you need.

After becoming grounded, leaders are ready to *explore new pathways,* the focus of the four chapters in part II. An extended discussion of the Struggle Lens provides context and texture as the exploring practices are examined:

- Reimagine the situation to discover a new creative path.

- Reinvent yourself.

- Overcome your blind spots.

- Heal yourself from conflict.

- Envision the common ground.

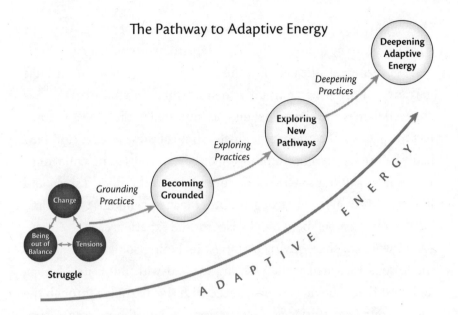

The Pathway to Adaptive Energy

- Write or revise your personal vision statement.

- Recommit, pivot, or leap.

Part III is dedicated to *deepening your adaptive energy* so that you can fully realize your leadership potential. The deepening practices offered in these final two chapters validate that the leadership journey is a marathon. Yet the journey becomes more enjoyable and rewarding with every mile as you learn and apply the deepening practices:

- Prepare for what lies ahead.

- Harness the engine of discipline.

- Celebrate what's precious.

Taking Center Stage: Leader Stories

A real-world exploration of leadership struggle requires real stories told by real leaders. You will meet people like Anne Mulcahy, Kathee Tesija, Ken Melrose, Joe Dowling, Dick Schulze, Marc Belton, Kate

Herzog, Joe Kelly, David Durenberger, and Mike Berman. All know what it's like to be highly regarded leaders in careers as diverse as business, government, theater, and the military. All share their struggle narratives and, more importantly, their learning. In a few stories I have changed names and altered details—as indicated in the Notes—to protect the privacy of certain individuals. Some of these leaders stumbled badly before recovering admirably to blaze new trails or imagine innovative new solutions. Others discovered more-fulfilling career and life paths through their struggles. Other leaders who nose-dived and burned out emerged better and wiser for the experience.

I will also share my own stories, including some that illustrate the lessons I learned while working for and with Bill Gates. I hope and trust that you will actively engage with this narrative through the use of your own stories as well, beginning with the reflective exercises in chapter 3 as well as the additional resources on my website, www.snyderleadership.com. By relating to and connecting with these leadership stories, taking the mastery practices to heart, and working through the accompanying exercises, you will make the art of struggle come to life in ways both personal and profound.

Fully investing in this book by treating it as an interactive experience can only benefit your own leadership journey. The art of struggle is messy and imprecise. The path is littered with obstacles. You must summon the courage to confront your own story, to reconstruct your leadership narrative, and to forge ahead even in the midst of hardship. Out of your discomfort will flow a newfound ease, a self-assuredness that is at once both calming and energizing, and the rewarding blend of command and confidence that only mastery can bestow.

If you are ready, it is time to begin.

Part I

Becoming Grounded

GROUNDING PRACTICES

Adopt a Growth Mind-Set

Become Resilient in the Face of Failure

Draw Your Tension Map

Center Your Mind, Body, and Spirit

Find the Support You Need

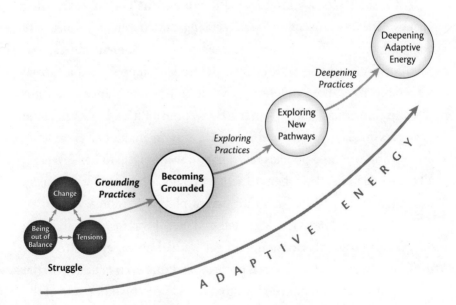

1

Struggle Is Not a Four-Letter Word

Heaven knows we need never be ashamed of our tears, for
they are rain upon the blinding dust of earth, overlying our
hard hearts. I was better after I had cried, than before—more
sorry, more aware of my own ingratitude, more gentle.

— Charles Dickens, *Great Expectations*

RITA MARSHALL'S TALENTS FOR CRAFTING GREAT PUBLIC RELA-
tions (PR) campaigns propelled her into a managerial position by the
age of 30. Soon after arriving at her new company, she encountered
her first leadership struggle.

Marshall was working as a PR professional in an advertising
agency. The two disciplines—advertising and public relations—are
very different, with dissimilar business models, nomenclatures, and
rhythms for engaging with clients. Before she stepped into a formal
leadership role, these differences, while minor annoyances, had not
directly concerned her. With her new responsibilities, however, came
new pressures. Now she had to find a way to make her company's
advertising-oriented policies relevant and meaningful to her PR team,
all the while motivating them to achieve results. She found it especially
challenging to be working with different players, customs, and rules.

During our interview Marshall told me: "I was tasked with being
a leader to grow this division, and yet we had an Excel grid to track
projects and progress and touch points that didn't even match up to the
types of projects and deliverables that we had on the other side of the
business. Even the words were different. You want your team focused

on the work and the deliverables for the client, and yet they were getting caught up in internal details for administering the business."

Greatly outnumbered, and with an advertising-oriented boss who had a different view of public relations, Marshall started to feel disillusioned and alone. Her boss began to cast doubt on her leadership, which caused her to doubt herself: "There was a point where I just thought, *Maybe I'm crazy. Maybe I don't know what I'm doing. Maybe they shouldn't put me out there in front of clients. I guess I just don't have it.* And that's a very frustrating thing when you're trying to lead, when you have self-doubts and your team is looking to you."

Marshall's self-doubts made matters worse. She found it difficult to lead with conviction and became frustrated with a culture that seemed to be blocking her progress. She had to do something. But what?

The Paradox of the Positive

Over the past several decades, the positive psychology movement has gained considerable momentum. It cascades into all areas of life—at work, with friends, in the community—subtly (and at times not so subtly), nudging a positive spin. All in all this is a good thing. Positive energy begets more positive energy. And numerous psychological studies show that when people feel optimistic and confident, they approach life with more vigor, have more-pleasant relationships, and are just plain happier.

Yet the full-throated emphasis on the positive comes at a price. The way that many organizational cultures internalize the principles of positive psychology actually undermines the very intentions of the movement. Indeed, positive psychology does not advocate ignoring the daunting life challenges that other branches of psychology attempt to treat; it is simply a call to pay as much attention to strengths as psychologists have historically given to weaknesses. This "be positive at all costs" misinterpretation can trigger unintentional consequences as it seeps into the cultural bloodstream. For instance, tuning out all negative thoughts and emotions can be a roadblock to the honest conversations people need to have with themselves and with others.

The parallels between cultural attitudes toward positivity and the view of struggle are striking. Like anything other than perpetual cheerfulness, struggle is commonly seen as a sign of weakness, a notion reinforced through a labyrinth of implicit messages. Many leaders unconsciously categorize the word *struggle* as negative and off-putting, a taboo, which makes dealing with struggle even more difficult than it needs to be.

This can become especially problematic when leaders find themselves facing significant challenges. When external pressures for positive spin create dissonance with reality, leaders may ignore the incongruity they feel in their guts and stifle the candid conversations that could guide them forward. They may unconsciously compare themselves with others and allow this comparison to diminish their self-image and curb their potential. They may fall into the trap of thinking that leaders are supposed to be perfect—or at least perfectly capable of dealing with struggle. Consequently, they can feel embarrassed and stigmatized, thinking, *Something must be wrong with me. I'm not like all the other successful leaders out there.*

But of course no leader is perfect. All human beings have their own unique flaws and frailties. And of course struggle is a natural part of leadership. Dick Schulze, founder and former CEO of consumer electronics giant Best Buy, who built the company to more than $50 billion in sales with over 180,000 employees, said it best when he told me: "I don't think that there has been a year in my 45 with the company that hasn't been beset with struggle."

Schulze then added:

With every episode of struggle, there is a learning opportunity.

Resolving the Paradox

The solution to the positivity paradox is relatively simple, but it demands a leap of faith. Instead of denying struggle, or feeling some degree of shame, savvy leaders embrace struggle as an opportunity for growth and learning, as an art to be mastered. They come to see struggle as a universal rite of passage without allowing themselves to become mired in it. They trust that engaging earnestly with struggle will ultimately take them to a better place, heightening their awareness of themselves and others and opening their minds to possibilities they may not have otherwise imagined.

Examples abound of prominent leaders who fail in a specific pursuit but who emerge stronger and more resilient from the experience. Had it not been for President John F. Kennedy's failure in the 1961 Bay of Pigs invasion, he might not have gained the wisdom needed to meet the greatest challenge of his presidency 18 months later: the Cuban Missile Crisis, which imperiled the very survival of the human race.

Clearly, struggle and leadership are intertwined. Teaming the courage to confront conflict with openness to new learning and the energy of positive thinking can turn struggle into transformation, paving the way for accelerated growth and development. The more that leaders move away from negative stereotypes and welcome a new relationship with struggle, the more they leave room for new possibilities to emerge. They begin asking better questions and recognizing the positive aspects of struggle. Shedding old assumptions, they free themselves to engage differently with the world around them, shaping their conversations to be more open and adaptive.

Two Stories of Struggle

Allow me to introduce you to two remarkable leaders whose struggle stories are vastly different. One was thrust into a top leadership job during a time of crisis; the other strove to fulfill a vision so ambitious and far-reaching that it seemed beyond the scope of human achievement.

Anne Mulcahy

In 2008 Anne Mulcahy was named CEO of the Year by *Chief Executive* magazine for her work at Xerox Corporation. Eight years earlier few would have predicted it.

In May 2000 Xerox was in turmoil. The board had abruptly fired G. Richard Thoman as CEO after a very brief tenure and brought back his predecessor, Paul Allaire, who personally recruited Mulcahy as president/chief operating officer (COO). By October, Mulcahy began to understand just how bad things were. Third-quarter earnings had missed analysts' expectations, and the company was close to declaring bankruptcy. Mulcahy candidly remarked on an October 3 investor conference call, "Xerox's business model is unsustainable." That simple comment sent the stock price nose-diving and set the stage for an extraordinary story of leadership growth and corporate transformation.

Shortly after that conference call, Mulcahy needed to make one of the most important decisions of her career: whether to seek bankruptcy protection or try to reverse the hemorrhaging of cash that was pushing the company close to insolvency. The company's financial advisers strongly recommended the bankruptcy route, but Mulcahy had a different vision. She felt bankruptcy would tarnish the reputation of the venerable company she had come to dearly love over her 25 years of employment there.

Instead, Mulcahy set the company down a path of pruning expenses and selling off business units, all the while preserving core assets essential to the rebuilding efforts. One of the core assets she preserved was the company's fledgling color-printing and copying business. In 2000 large-scale color printing was still in its infancy, but Mulcahy placed a big bet that the ensuing decade would see huge growth. She was right. By 2007, 40 percent of Xerox's total revenue would come from color printing, and Xerox products would capture the highest market share.

Early in her tenure as president/COO, Mulcahy met personally with key customers and the company's top 100 leaders, sharing her passion and enthusiasm and convincing them to remain loyal during this difficult time. She told her sales force: "I will go anywhere, anytime, to save a Xerox customer."

Her mission was nothing short of "restoring Xerox to a great company once again." But the path to get there would be dogged with adversity. "There were many near-death moments when we weren't sure the company could get through the crisis," she admitted.

Not only was the company's survival at stake but the struggle cut to the very core of Mulcahy's identity. "One day I had just flown back from Japan," she said. "I came back to the office and found it had been a dismal day. At around 8:30 p.m. on my way home, I pulled over to the side of the Merritt Parkway and said to myself, *I don't know where to go. I don't want to go home. There's just no place to go.*"

In the midst of her despair, Mulcahy checked her voice mail and found a supportive message from one of her colleagues telling her how much everyone believed in her and the company. "That was all I needed to just drive home, and get up again the next morning," she said.

Mulcahy's leadership growth is even more remarkable when you consider her background. She had come through the ranks in sales, spent time in human resources, and had just become the general manager of a small, out-of-the-way business unit when she was tapped for the role of president/COO.

One of the most intriguing aspects of Mulcahy's background is that she had very little financial training. She had never held a financial management job and felt clearly over her head as she navigated the hostile financial waters of disappointing earnings, stock market declines, and angry analysts.

Mulcahy's untimely remark during the October 3, 2000, investor conference call is a good example of her financial inexperience. Her bold statement that Xerox's business model was unsustainable may have been accurate, although there were undoubtedly more market-sensitive ways to communicate Xerox's shaky financial status while still remaining authentic as a leader.

Fortunately, Mulcahy sought out capable mentors who helped her recover from that early misstep. In 2002, a year after being promoted to CEO, she personally renegotiated a $7 billion revolving line of credit, pulling together a consortium of 58 banks that needed to approve the deal. In the process she went toe to toe with Citigroup CEO Sandy Weill, successfully securing his commitment to personally reel in three holdout banks.

Mulcahy would summarize her experience as follows: "This was a job that would dramatically change my life, requiring every ounce of energy that I had. I never expected to be CEO, nor was I groomed for it."

Bill Gates

In marked contrast to Anne Mulcahy, Bill Gates envisioned himself as a CEO at a very young age, and at every step in his career he took proactive measures to hone the skills he needed to actualize his vision.

I began working closely with Bill Gates in 1983, when I served as Microsoft's liaison with IBM. At 28 I was just a year older than Bill. Microsoft, like the personal computer industry itself, was gaining traction. Still, with just $50 million in revenue and 250 employees, it was light years away from becoming the $74 billion behemoth it is today.

About two years into my tenure, Steve Ballmer, Bill Gates, and I were on an airplane flying back to Seattle from a successful meeting with IBM in Boca Raton. Bill and Steve were sitting together; I was a few rows forward with an empty seat next to me. In the middle of the flight, Bill came over to sit with me. After briefly talking about our development tools business, he asked me to become the general manager of the group.

I knew what a big deal that was to Bill. He was entrusting me with the company's legacy. Microsoft got its start back in 1975 when Bill Gates and Paul Allen wrote the first BASIC Interpreter (one of the products in the development tools area) and licensed it to MITS on the first personal computer, the Altair.

By 1985 Microsoft's product line had blossomed into a number of programming languages, including Assembler, BASIC, C, COBOL, Fortran, and Pascal. But its business had come under fire by an upstart called Borland International. Borland sold more than 500,000 units of Turbo Pascal and became the dominant player in that market, decimating our Pascal business. All of us knew that it was just a matter of time before Borland would launch an assault on our C product as well as on our flagship BASIC.

Putting me in charge of this group meant that Bill had crossed a psychological hurdle that he had wrestled with for a while. He knew that as our businesses evolved, it would be necessary to appoint general managers who could oversee all aspects of product strategy, marketing, and development. This new cadre of leaders would have the skills to formulate business strategy, assess market threats and opportunities, evaluate strategic alternatives, and focus resources on the most productive path.

But there was one problem. It would mean violating what Bill held as almost a sacred principle of leadership. Bill's name for this violation was the "inverted hierarchy," a situation in which a technical manager reports to a boss who is less technically qualified. Its very name implies that something is topsy-turvy.

Bill's reason for respecting the sanctity of the technical hierarchy stemmed from his core belief that the best way to motivate software engineers was to have them supervised by people who were more technically qualified, whom they would learn from and respect. This model had worked extremely well for Microsoft in the decade since its inception.

Bill had begun to rethink this approach a year earlier, when he created two divisions—the Applications Division and the Systems Division—each core to Microsoft's business at the time. He put his trusted college friend Steve Ballmer in charge of the Systems Division, while Bill led the Applications Division himself. Creating a business unit for our development tools business meant pushing the inverted hierarchy down one more level. While Bill knew of the risks involved, he could also see the competitive landscape unfolding with Borland. If he did not act, Borland would wreak havoc when it invaded Microsoft's turf of C and BASIC.

When I look back, I now understand the intuitive leap of faith that Bill took to make this move. Technical excellence was at the core of Microsoft's competitive strategy, and its software engineers were Microsoft's crown jewel. Now Bill would need to give up a key aspect of his leadership model that had driven the company's success for its first decade.

I would observe numerous other examples of Bill's growth as a leader as we continued to work together over the next several years. One such example came as we were preparing the launch plans for our new BASIC and C products in 1987, launches that would leapfrog Borland with potentially game-changing innovations.

Part of our plan was to tap into the energy of computer user groups, whose members were key influencers in the fledgling market for development tools. Knowing how much excitement Steve Jobs generated when he unveiled the Macintosh in 1984 at the Boston Computer Society, I envisioned Bill as our keynote speaker. I figured we could easily draw 1,500 people at a launch event, quickly building momentum.

We were well into our launch planning, and I noticed that Bill had not yet agreed to speak. His reluctance was puzzling to me. I wondered, *What are his concerns? What could possibly be holding him back?* To me this was such an obvious strategy. Bill was a brilliant speaker.

He had a unique way of combining clarity of message, eloquence of delivery, and passion, with a nice dollop of humor.

Bill and I would meet informally for brainstorming sessions from time to time, so at one meeting I finally asked him about it. His concerns seemed to center around Q&A: What if someone asked a question to which he didn't know the answer?

I tried to encourage him. I told him that he was a very effective speaker, and I could not imagine a single question he could not answer. Also, our lead technical guru would be sitting in the front row in case there was a need for further elaboration.

I guess that small measure of reassurance was enough. Bill agreed to speak, and we introduced our new C product at the Boston Computer Society in front of more than 1,700 people. Of course Bill gave a magnificent speech. The Q&A went well, too. On one question, Bill looked tentatively in our direction, as if to check himself, but he had already given a solid answer and there was no need to say anything more. The launch was a huge success, as was the launch of our new BASIC when Bill spoke to the Philadelphia user group several weeks later. Microsoft would go on to defeat Borland and regain its dominance in the market.

I would never again talk to Bill about the concerns he expressed that day. There was no need; he had successfully crossed the threshold. But now, thinking about the episode many years later, I remember how many steps Bill took to come up to speed on our products before the launch. By the multitude of questions he had fired off via e-mail, it was clear that he had thoroughly pored over all the technical material he had requested. By the time he spoke, he had taken the time to fully prepare himself to answer almost anything.

Three Defining Elements of Leadership Struggle

Struggle occurs when a difficult or complex situation arises that presents some challenge or adversity. The details can vary considerably—from beginning a new job or confronting a major disappointment to facing a difficult decision or managing an unexpected external event—but in all examples there are three fundamental conditions that determine the nature of the struggle and serve as its defining elements: change, tensions, and being out of balance.

Defining Elements of Struggle

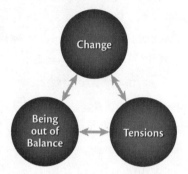

Change

Change stands at the heart of leadership struggle. Every struggle is triggered by some type of change. Perhaps a leader initiates that change by envisioning a new direction for the organization; struggle may emerge from forces that stand in opposition to that vision. In other cases change may be imposed on a leader by a new set of enterprise-related circumstances caused by loss of key personnel, financial constraints, competitive pressures, or some other setback. Large-scale changes such as economic recession or cultural upheaval may produce more-serious, long-term consequences.

External change, whether desired or not, always carries with it seeds of opportunity and growth. The struggle may come from discerning the best way to take advantage of those opportunities or how to do so with limited resources.

Even when change is welcome, struggle is often a natural by-product. A move to a new job or company can be exciting, yet it requires a step outside the comfort zone into a puzzling new world that has yet to be comprehended much less mastered.

In still other cases, change comes from deep within a leader's inner world. As the heart and the mind expand to take in new ideas, feelings, and perspectives, struggle comes from the process of clarifying newly emerging values and identity.

In Anne Mulcahy's story, change is the central theme on multiple fronts. Xerox needed to dramatically alter its course; otherwise it would spin into bankruptcy. The industry was also changing, opening a door of opportunity to capitalize on the emergence of large-scale commercial color printing. Finally, Mulcahy herself needed to change and grow as a leader to rise to the challenge.

The Bill Gates stories I've shared can also be understood in the context of his audacious vision of change. When he founded Microsoft in 1975 at age 19, he boldly envisioned that there would be a computer on every desk and in every home and that every computer would run Microsoft software. During my five years at Microsoft, his energies centered on actualizing this dream. At a company meeting in late 1987, Bill announced that we were about halfway there. Hearing this I made a mental note that the year 2000 would carry some significance. As it turned out, that was the year that Bill elevated Steve Ballmer to be the second CEO of Microsoft, freeing Bill to eventually embark on his new journey as full-time philanthropist. In this new role, Bill would turn his attention to bringing about a new wave of societal changes and innovations, ranging from education and health care to energy and global development.

Tensions

The process of change creates a natural set of tensions, the second defining element of leadership struggle. Chapter 4 offers a detailed look at the four tension points that grow out of struggle. These tension points stem from individual and institutional traditions (past) and aspirations (future) as well as (outward) relationships and (inward) identity.

Being out of Balance

The third element of leadership struggle is that change and its ensuing tensions throw a leader off balance. Sometimes the imbalance is felt in subtle ways: a quiet voice, a nagging concern in the leader's gut, or reluctance or procrastination of an important task. Sometimes the fears are deeper, the emotions more powerful. A leader may lose confidence and feel the weight of the world on his or her shoulders. Some individuals remain cool and collected at work and unleash all their frustration on their families when they get home. Still others may vent their stress in self-defeating behaviors like gambling or drinking, all the while denying that a problem exists.

One female leader shared a harrowing experience while working as a brand manager at a major consumer products company: "It was so stressful. My hair started falling out. I didn't realize it was stress. All I knew was I could see my scalp in the mirror when I brushed my teeth. It was hard. It was really hard. It was joyless."

Other leaders had these recollections:

- "It was incredibly difficult. If I had to name the emotions, I would say anger, hurt, and betrayal were right on top."

- "Fear. I had fear. I had anger. I think I went through everything. I had sadness."

- "Frustration. You don't feel like your voice is being heard anymore. And I had a very influential voice before."

- "There were periods when I would be sleep deprived. And it's really hard to deal with pressure when you are sleep deprived."

- "I didn't have peace. When your job is extra stressful, you are always thinking about it. Your mind is preoccupied. You start to focus on that, and you keep thinking about it: *How can I make it better? How can I fix it? How can I change? Is there a way out? Are there any other possibilities?* You start questioning and asking all these questions. If it's giving you so much stress that it's affecting the rest of your life, it's not good. That's what I call not having peace."

An important note: A leader may *be* out of balance without actually *being aware* that he or she is out of balance. Very often family members, friends, life partners, and colleagues are more keenly aware of the imbalance than is the one going through the struggle. Other people's willingness and courage to confront someone they care about, and that person's willingness to listen, can be major steps in resolving the struggle. A leader's acknowledgment and awareness of being out of balance is central to regaining balance and becoming centered again.

Playing Out Struggle: Scripts

Leaders respond to the change, tension, and intense emotions of their struggles in different ways. I have identified six scripts that describe different progressions in a struggle episode. By understanding these scripts, leaders gain the agility to shift course midstream or even to proactively select a script in advance, circumventing problems that might otherwise have surfaced. Here is a brief introduction to each of the scripts, which we explore in more detail in upcoming stories.

Script #1: Proactive Reinvention

In the proactive-reinvention script, leaders recognize that strategies that may have worked in the past are no longer effective. Reinvention—the willingness to start anew with a fresh perspective—is required in order to forge new strategies that are more adaptive to the current circumstances. For example, Bill Gates reinvented a crucial aspect of his leadership model when he accepted the need for an "inverted hierarchy." He also proactively took steps to overcome his fears, agreeing to assume the important role of product spokesperson at user group events during Microsoft's battle for market share with Borland.

Script #2: Stumble, Recover, and Learn

After making mistakes due to inexperience, leaders who follow the stumble/recover/learn script recognize those errors and take appropriate corrective action. They also strive to repair any relationships that were damaged along the way and vow never again to repeat the pattern. This was Anne Mulcahy's script, which began when she declared Xerox's business model unsustainable on an investor conference call in October 2000.

Script #3: Burnout

Passionate leaders with bold ideas may enthusiastically charge ahead in new situations, all fired up to do whatever it takes to realize their vision. But as the burnout script progresses, they encounter stakeholders who do not share their enthusiasm or their vision. These hard-charging leaders are often so convinced that their vision is superior that they fail to take the time to fully understand and appreciate anyone else's point of view. Consequently, when their colleagues have very different ideas, the stage is set for conflict. All too often relationships are soured and enemies are made. Yet instead of stepping back to consider their role in the conflict, such leaders tend to blame others, whom they clearly see as wrong. Inevitably, their past actions restrict their future options, and they find themselves trapped in situations in which they have little control. They not only feel drained of physical and emotional energy but fail to realize how their attitude and behavior drain the energy of others as well. Ultimately, they either leave in exhaustion or are fired. This script played out for Steve Jobs during his first tenure at Apple.

Script #4: Transcending Constraint

In the transcending-constraint script, leaders initially see tremendous obstacles ahead but feel incapable of surmounting them due to external constraints. As their adaptive energy kicks in, however, they begin reimagining the situation, revealing strategies and options that had previously escaped their awareness. This is how Rita Marshall's script plays out in the next section.

Script #5: Mission Impossible

At first the mission-impossible script feels similar to the transcending-constraint script. The difference is, no matter how creative and dedicated these leaders may be, every road toward resolution comes to a dead end. Ultimately, they are forced to accept that there is no way to realize their vision and aspirations. The constraints are simply insurmountable. If leaving is not an option, they are reduced to hunkering down while trying to maintain some degree of balance.

Script #6: Confronting Failure

In the confronting-failure script, leaders are forced to acknowledge that things did not work out according to their plans and expectations. In a word, they have *failed*. The struggle is finding ways to remain resilient as they pick themselves up, dust themselves off, and move on while still learning from the experience. This was the Steve Jobs script after he lost the power struggle at Apple in 1985.

A Lifelong Journey

Rita Marshall, who attempted to lead the PR function in an advertising agency, most closely follows the transcending-constraint script.

Marshall relied on her natural optimism to quickly help her regain her balance. She found the inner strength to search for a creative solution, tapping into the very tensions that were causing her distress. She was concerned about how she could lead with conviction and authenticity when people seemed to doubt she had the expertise to do the job. So she took action to increase her credibility by pursuing professional accreditation in public relations. Achieving this accreditation was a "big deal" to Marshall; it boosted her confidence and provided external validation of her PR expertise to her doubting boss.

Furthermore, Marshall's sense of isolation was a stressor. While she felt a professional kinship with the people working for her, it was inappropriate and counterproductive to confide in them. She felt her boss was unable to provide her with the support she needed, so Marshall proactively created an external support system. First she tapped into her family, but soon she found camaraderie at PR professional associations and peer women's support groups. Ultimately, she found a mentor who had the experience and the wisdom she was seeking.

These actions gave Marshall the confidence she needed to improve her effectiveness and transcend the constraints she may have initially felt were insurmountable. Over time she learned to appreciate the differences between advertising and public relations and saw how they could work together rather than in opposition.

Marshall and I spoke again about a year after our initial interview. After working for a long time within an advertising culture, she had decided to build on her knowledge and experience by starting her own PR firm. This did not surprise me. Now in her forties, Marshall had reached what author Gail Sheehy has called "the age of mastery," a time when people's professional skills solidify and they feel a sense of confidence in what they can contribute to the world.

But there was also a twist in Marshall's story. For months she had been watching her 19-year-old son slide deeper into drug addiction. She and her family were entering a new chapter in their lives as they learned to cope with this difficult challenge. Marshall shared with me an essay she wrote that was published in a local newspaper:

> Our son's addiction called into consideration my beliefs and values. It had been a long time since faith and spirituality played a

significant role in my life, but if ever there was a good time to reconnect, this was it.

Some things remain a struggle, but I embrace the journey for what it is and choose my actions and perspective. There have been some incredibly bright spots, including meeting people whom I genuinely admire but might never have met, developing more meaningful relationships with friends and family, reconnecting with a higher power, and engaging some of my gifts, including advocacy and writing.

One of the most remarkable findings from my research was how people's perceptions of struggle evolve over time. Leaders I interviewed often recalled stories that had occurred two, three, or even four decades earlier. As these leaders reflected on the impact that their struggles had on their lives, they acknowledged that the passage of time had given them a broader perspective.

Remember the brand manager who was so stressed that her hair was falling out? She got through her ordeal and eventually became the CEO of a different company. Here is how she reflected on the totality of her experiences: "From my perspective, every single bump in the road, slap in the face, knee in the back—every single one of those things was a fabulous gift. You get through it, and you stop and say, 'That hurt like hell, what was that?' And you say, 'Oh, my gosh, I am in this bright, sunny place as a result.' There isn't a single one of those things that I don't reflect on as a gift of some form."

In the midst of a major crisis, it may be hard to think of such difficult challenges as gifts. But with the healing that comes with time, it is natural for people to alter their perceptions. This process becomes self-reinforcing. The more we think of bumps, slaps, and knees in the back as gifts, or at least as opportunities for growth and learning, the more capably we can handle whatever life sends our way.

In the words of Rita Marshall, "I don't think any of us wakes up in the morning and says, 'I hope I have a struggle today.'" Still there are times when struggle is inevitable. At these times leaders need to recognize what is unfolding around them, adapt their energy accordingly, and make informed, well-reasoned choices. Indeed adaptive energy is a vital and necessary force that leaders need to harness if they are to realize their aspirations. This becomes clearer in the next chapter through the leadership examples of Kate Herzog, Bill Gates, and Steve Jobs.

Adaptive Energy

Okonkwo's fear . . . was not external
but lay deep within himself.

— Chinua Achebe, *Things Fall Apart*

Creating a Luxury Beach Resort in Ghana

Even though Anne Mulcahy was unprepared for her role as president/
COO of Xerox, at least she was able to draw from a long history of
career success. For Kate Herzog the sudden demands of a daunting
new role came early. Still untested, Herzog summoned every ounce
of adaptive energy to meet and conquer her challenges with ingenuity
and resourcefulness.

Herzog grew up in a small village in Ghana, West Africa. When
she was a child, an anthropologist visited her village. Determined to
learn how to speak and read English, Herzog saw her opportunity and
persuaded the anthropologist to help. He gave her an anthology of the
comic *The Adventures of Tintin*. Herzog would travel with Tintin and
his dog Snowy to all the corners of the world. She told me: "Books
opened many doors for me. They took me from my world in that tiny
village to an entirely magical world. It made it okay for me to dream."

Dreaming would pay off for Herzog. When she was 27, she found
her way to the consulting division of Deloitte & Touche in Ghana,
where she started as a business analyst, the lowest rung on the consulting ladder. Soon she noticed that she was not like the majority of her
colleagues, who were educated at prestigious universities around the
world. Herzog had never been outside Ghana.

Herzog first worked on a telecommunications project. When that went well, she was asked to write a report summarizing the issues facing a struggling beachfront resort hotel. The hotel was owned by a married couple who had hired members from both sides of their family to operate the hotel. These family members did not always get along. Said Herzog, "So, you have the family members from the husband's side and the family members from the wife's side all put in one pot, where everybody is trying to have a stick in the ground—everybody's trying to have the upper hand. It was just a mess."

Herzog's report was simple and straightforward, just two or three pages—not the usual Deloitte & Touche expanse. "There is a family feud going on there, and that is a path to disaster," she wrote. Her solution was equally simple: fire all the family members and hire managers from outside the family.

Herzog was shocked by what happened next. The owners arranged with Deloitte for Herzog to run the hotel on a consulting basis. They wanted her to turn their chaotic operation, where "employees would steal chickens, plates, sheets, towels, whatever"—into a first-rate beach resort.

Herzog had never worked in a hotel; in fact, she had never even slept in one. Nor had she ever managed a business of any kind: "At Deloitte I worked in collaboration with other consultants, who were extremely smart and knew what they were doing. Now I had to go run a hotel."

She frantically searched for a successful model for guidance. She gathered several hotel employees and drove to the big city to see what a successful hotel might look like. She remembers other hotel employees wondering aloud why the trip was necessary. After all, she was supposed to be the expert; everyone expected her to just tell them what to do. Herzog knew that this was a common perception among Deloitte clients. Her firm was paid a lot of money, and people expected the consultant to have all the answers. Such unrealistic expectations only intensified Herzog's fear: "I was scared of losing my job. Unemployment in Ghana was over 30 percent. And I was going on a path that could jeopardize my work."

As Herzog got to know the people who were now working for her, she found one person who seemed to know what she was doing. She appointed this woman as her assistant, putting her in charge of the hotel's operations.

Herzog had a picture in her mind, a grand vision of what she wanted the hotel to become: "This has to be a place that people should always want to come back to because of what we do well. We create good food. We create a good environment. It is clean. It is wonderful. It is paradise."

Herzog summed up the hotel's value proposition in five simple words: *We create memories worth repeating.* Things headed on an upward path. More customers came to the hotel, and they returned a second and third time. The financial results improved.

This continued for about a year. Gradually, Herzog realized that her assistant, while well versed on hotel operations, was stifling the other employees with her controlling management style. Herzog felt that the woman was acting more and more like a bully and was hurting the team's morale. Herzog told me, "I was so dependent on her. I was not using other people like I should." Herzog knew that she needed to take some control back, which was met by stiff resistance from her assistant, who threatened to quit. Fortunately, by this time Herzog was feeling much more confident. With the blessing of the hotel owners, she let her assistant resign.

"And that is when the magic started happening," Herzog told me. She regularly called all 70 employees together, just like the custom of the village where she grew up. At first the employees complained, but then they started coming up with their own ideas for improvements. Soon a new culture was thriving. Instead of feeling controlled by Herzog's proxy, people were feeling part of a vibrant, energized team.

Herzog implemented many of the employees' suggestions to create better working conditions. She offered all employees one free meal per day—a good hot meal using hotel ingredients. "They also got to take showers in a very beautiful tiled bathroom, just like a guest's bathroom," she noted. She implemented a policy to reward employees who were singled out by guests for outstanding service, with useful things to improve their lives like gas stoves, televisions, and refrigerators.

Soon the hotel achieved its goal. Under Herzog's leadership and the expert ways in which she wielded her adaptive energy, it became a luxury beach resort.

Adaptive Energy

As far back as her childhood, Herzog had demonstrated an ability to tap into her adaptive energy. Driven to learn English, she had stepped forward as soon as the opportunity presented itself. She then eagerly digested the Tintin books, which ignited her imagination and dreams.

When Herzog was asked to write a report about the hotel, she zeroed in on the problem, pinpointing in a very few pages the essence of the issue without the usual consulting fluff. With no prior experience, Herzog took the initiative to drive with her colleagues to the city to witness how a successful hotel operates. She found an assistant who could help her come up to speed. A year later she heeded critical feedback about that assistant and handled the situation confidently and professionally. Finally, fully in control, Herzog drew on her early life experiences with the power of village assemblies to harness the energy of every hotel employee.

Adaptive energy is the force that propels you to reach your dreams, pointing you toward the goal line and warning you when you veer off course. It aligns your actions both with the *external* criteria necessary for success and with your *inner* values and principles. Through adaptive energy you listen to and assess feedback from multiple sources and incorporate this new learning in future actions, all the while remaining true to yourself.

Harnessing adaptive energy can inspire you to come up with innovative ideas when no immediate solution is evident. It can also steer you to build lasting and fulfilling relationships. Even though your interactions might involve conflict, you gain the acuity and the agility to manage the conflict so that it does not stand in the way of what needs to be done.

This powerful force gives you the courage to persist when failure seems imminent, the resilience to bounce back from setbacks, and the strength of mind to resist being stuck or lost in negative thought patterns that could hold you back. Everyone has negative thoughts and bad moods, but leaders who can access their adaptive energy are able to channel their adverse emotions into creativity and goal-oriented pursuits. Doing so can propel you *and* your organization back into what author and psychology professor Mihaly Csikszentmihalyi calls "flow," that immersive mental state of energized focus in which attention is concentrated in positive and productive ways.

Perhaps the greatest adversary of adaptive energy is fear. Herzog acknowledged her fears but did not let them get in her way. She channeled all of her energy into the pursuit of her dreams. Even though she was young, inexperienced, and focused on her career aspirations, she was instinctively collaborative, even generous in her leadership. Her skill in leveraging her adaptive energy created an environment in which everyone did well, felt valued, and was fully invested in the mission.

Not all leaders manage to stay so positive. Some have difficulties pushing aside negative emotions so that their adaptive energy can surface. In such cases their energy may work against them, propelling them to take actions that can undermine their success and thwart their growth. That is the scenario that played out with Herzog's assistant. She could not get past her egotistical need to be in control; she dug in her heels and refused to change. In such situations, a leader may express energy through frustration, anger, hostility, or self-doubt, unwittingly harming the very relationships that are so important for success. Most often such leaders do not have the perspective to see the central role they played in the conflict.

A Study of Contrasts: Bill Gates and Steve Jobs

A good contrast of adaptive approaches can be found in the comparison between Bill Gates and Steve Jobs. Both captured the public's attention because of their genius, their maverick approaches, and their technical innovations. But they had very different journeys, with very different scripts. Gates was primarily identified with the proactive-reinvention script due to his skill at recognizing challenges that lay ahead and adjusting his leadership priorities accordingly.

Steve Jobs, on the other hand, walked a very different path. Jobs's professional life played out like a narrative in three acts: Steve Jobs 1.0, 2.0, and 3.0. Each of these acts unfolded according to a different script.

Steve Jobs 1.0: Burnout

At a time when Bill Gates was mobilizing Microsoft to achieve his vision, Steve Jobs was unconsciously, and probably unintentionally, tearing Apple apart. In one of his most destructive acts, he pitted the Lisa team against the Macintosh team. Due to his negative outbursts, he was stripped of his responsibilities for the Lisa development effort in 1980. Jobs then showed disdain for the Lisa team, openly calling them inferior. His final words of vitriol came as a quarter of the Lisa team was laid off in 1985. "You guys failed," he said, looking directly at those who had worked on the Lisa. "You're a B team. B players. Too many people here are B or C players, so today we are releasing some of you to have the opportunity to work at our sister companies here in the valley."

Jobs could not hide his disgust for CEO John Sculley, an animosity that would become his ultimate undoing. Jobs personally recruited

Sculley in 1983 and developed a seemingly close relationship with him. By 1985, however, Jobs's hostility had turned the relationship caustic, driving Sculley to do the unthinkable: mount a coup that would lead to Jobs's ouster.

This period of Jobs's career conforms to the burnout script. Undermining company objectives and ignoring all feedback and warning signals, the self-absorbed Jobs was such a net drain on employee morale and organizational energy that he could no longer positively contribute to the very corporation he had helped create.

Steve Jobs 2.0: Confronting Failure

Immediately after Jobs was stripped of his power, he reckoned with his new reality: confronting failure. According to Walter Isaacson's biography, "Jobs stayed home for the next few days, blinds drawn, his answering machine on, seeing only his girlfriend, Tina Redse. For hours on end he sat there playing his Bob Dylan tapes, especially 'The Times They Are a-Changin'.' He had recited the second verse the day he unveiled the Macintosh to the Apple shareholders sixteen months earlier. That verse ended: 'For the loser now / Will be later to win.'"

Jobs would later recall, "I felt like I'd been punched, the air knocked out of me and I couldn't breathe." He traveled to Europe and upon his return started another computer company called NeXT, its very name signaling the self-absorption that still ruled him. But through NeXT and Pixar (now the gold standard for computer animation film studios), Jobs grew in his understanding of himself and of leadership, and he learned how to apply those lessons at the intersection of liberal arts and technology. These ventures outside Apple were a prelude to his third and final act.

Steve Jobs 3.0: Proactive Reinvention

Steve Jobs 3.0 returned to Apple a changed, more self-aware man who no longer was his own worst enemy. He had harnessed his energy to be more adaptive. The essence of his reinvention is best understood through the Struggle Lens: he learned how "to make some important human values real and effective."

Steve Jobs 1.0 was driven by a singular and almost maniacal purpose: building "insanely great" products. But after rebooting twice, Steve Jobs 3.0 framed his passion differently: "to build an enduring company where people were motivated to make great products." This new articulation would give Jobs the space to mobilize his energies more effectively, with a longer-term aim in mind. He cultivated collaborative relationships with others who had critical skills he lacked, taking care to keep these individuals engaged and motivated. From the very beginning of his return to Apple, Jobs showed that, to a certain extent, he was willing to put aside his ego to accomplish a greater vision. Consider his humble and appreciative impromptu words at the 1997 Macworld Expo, announcing Microsoft's $150 million investment in Apple:

> If we want to move forward, and see Apple healthy and prospering again, we have to let go of a few things here. We have to let go of this notion that for Apple to win, Microsoft has to lose. We have to embrace a notion that for Apple to win, Apple has to do a really good job. And if others are going to help us, that's great, because we need all the help we can get. And if we screw up and we don't do a good job, it's not somebody else's fault. It's our fault. So I think that's a very important perspective. If we want Microsoft Office on the Mac, we better treat the company that puts it out with a little bit of gratitude. We like their software. So the era of setting this up as a competition between Apple and Microsoft is over as far as I'm concerned. This is about getting Apple healthy, and this is about Apple being able to make incredibly great contributions to the industry and to get healthy and prosper again.

Channeling Adaptive Energy through Self-Awareness

All leaders have the potential to channel their energy in ways that are adaptive and aligned with their purpose. How they do that is the central question, which is answered gradually as you read through these pages. As an art, leadership struggle cannot be reduced to a single sound bite or simple formula, but a key concept is this: *the more self-aware you are, the more capable you will be of adaptively channeling your behavior.* Leaders who wish to become more self-aware need to understand the nature of their automatic and reflective minds.

The Automatic and Reflective Minds

In the book *Thinking, Fast and Slow*, Daniel Kahneman paints a portrait of two personalities of thought. One personality is the fast mind, which Kahneman calls System 1; the other is a slower mind, called System 2. Kahneman did not assign names to these two minds. To make them easier to remember and relate to, think of them as the automatic mind and the reflective mind.

The *automatic mind,* the faster one, reaches judgments and conclusions quickly but often prematurely, making associations with information already stored and easily accessible. Its methods for reaching these conclusions are often not subject to conscious awareness, leaving a person with a gut feeling that it "seems right." The automatic mind is eager to satisfy the need for order and understanding but is prone to mistakes stemming from the zeal to move quickly and decisively. It is overconfident, resisting calls from the reflective mind to slow down. Many people intuitively call it "automatic pilot," with the connotation that decisions are made routinely, out of habit, subject to preprogrammed routines. In the mindfulness tradition, it is known as "monkey mind."

The *reflective mind* is slower and more methodical. It is capable of reason, logic, and metathought—the process of consciously observing one's own thought process, as if looking down on oneself from the balcony. It challenges assumptions, generates multiple alternatives and evaluates them systematically, and is capable of objective analysis. It is the spark for conscious and intentional action. But it has one big problem: it tends to be lazy, often ceding control to the automatic mind, which can lead to regrettable consequences. If the automatic mind is the mind of habit, the reflective mind helps break free of old habits to form new and better ones.

Consider the following question:

A bat and ball cost $1.10.
The bat costs one dollar more than the ball.
How much does the ball cost?

If you are like most people, the first thing that popped into your mind is "10 cents." Your automatic mind supplied this answer quickly and effortlessly. But is it correct? If the ball costs 10 cents, that would make the bat $1.10, which comes to a total of $1.20.

If you do the math:

$$x + (x + 1.00) = 1.10$$

you find that x (the ball) is actually 5 cents. That makes the bat $1.05 and the grand total $1.10.

If you came up with the wrong answer, you are in good company. Kahneman reports that more than half of students at Harvard, Princeton, and the Massachusetts Institute of Technology failed to answer this seemingly trivial problem correctly.

What happened? The automatic mind, certain that "10 cents" is the correct answer, tells the reflective mind not to bother. The reflective mind, lazy one that it is, quickly acquiesces.

The automatic mind, which tends to be defensive, may dismiss this as a trivial example. Who cares whether the ball costs a nickel or a dime? The stakes are negligible. Yet these types of errors occur all the time on a much larger scale, sometimes with devastating consequences. Two independent streams of research conclude that relying too heavily on your automatic mind can leave you unnecessarily vulnerable to costly errors. The first research thread centers on emotional intelligence.

One reason for the failure of Steve Jobs 1.0 was that he was unable to control his emotions. His outrage and disdain would reach such intensity that they demanded release; unfortunately, he consistently chose to verbalize them, which strained his relationships and undermined company objectives. Jobs apparently had no insight into the damage he was doing, suggesting that he did not pay adequate attention to the subtle (and perhaps not so subtle) social cues and feedback that could have alerted him that something was amiss. His automatic mind had run amok.

Daniel Goleman's work on emotional intelligence shows that the reflective mind can be trained to filter and edit the workings of the automatic mind to better manage emotions. Even though he would never be considered a warm and caring person, Steve Jobs 3.0 did manage to sufficiently modulate his emotions, temper counterproductive outbursts, and even occasionally express humility, thus channeling his emotions to align with his higher, more inclusive aspirations.

A second research stream, championed by psychologist Keith Stanovich, is relatively new. Stanovich focuses on a different aspect of automatic-mind vulnerability where rational processes break down and thinking becomes distorted, convoluted, and prone to error. While Goleman's work centers on emotional and social well-being, Stanovich focuses squarely on goal-directed thinking. In his book *What Intelligence Tests Miss: The Psychology of Rational Thought*, Stanovich posits that a goal-directed rational thinker tends to:

- Seek various points of view before coming to a conclusion

- Think extensively about a problem before responding

- Think about future consequences before taking action

- Calibrate the degree of strength of one's opinion to the degree of evidence available

- Seek nuance and avoid absolutism

Steve Jobs is often celebrated for his "reality distortion field," the notion that he could bend reality to suit his own purposes. But Steve Jobs 1.0 violated every one of Stanovich's guidelines when, in a power struggle with John Sculley, he miscalculated the degree and the extent to which the Apple Board of Directors would support him. His egotistical and self-absorbed automatic mind had contorted and distorted reality beyond the breaking point.

The wiser and retooled Steve Jobs 3.0 leveraged a more finely calibrated reality distortion field, not solely to champion his own greatness but also to motivate and inspire others to achieve great things. While the more enlightened Jobs still strove to bend reality to his will, he did so while hewing more to Stanovich's parameters, relying on his trusted confidants for input. When he pushed too hard and too far, he learned from his mistakes and was less likely to repeat them.

In the end, perhaps aided by the insights he gained through the practice of Soto Zen Buddhist meditation, Jobs became a master of adaptive action. He learned to temper the bluster of his automatic mind by training his two minds—automatic and reflective—to work synergistically together. This is the hallmark of great leaders. With experience, they nurture their reflective mind to be more proactive and sagelike while training their automatic mind to increase its associative powers, thereby generating richer and more creative ideas for the reflective mind to consider.

You can learn how to do this as well. The exercises in the next chapter will help get you started.

3

Turn Your Energy into Adaptive Energy

It's the chance of a lifetime
In a lifetime of chance
And it's high time you joined
In the dance

— Dan Fogelberg, "Run for the Roses"

THE STORIES OF BILL GATES, STEVE JOBS, ANNE MULCAHY, RITA Marshall, and Kate Herzog have illustrated the key foundational concepts of leadership struggle: defining elements, scripts, adaptive energy, and the reflective and automatic minds. It is now time to put these concepts to work by intentionally building your capacity for adaptive action. The grounding practices in part I form the bedrock for regaining balance, getting your perspective in sync with the reality of what you are facing, and becoming more emotionally and spiritually centered.

The first grounding practice, which serves as the cornerstone for all the rest, encourages you to make a subtle yet powerful shift in your worldview, a step toward making your leadership journey more productive, fulfilling, and enjoyable.

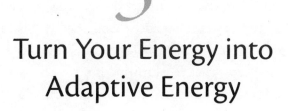

GROUNDING PRACTICE

Adopt a Growth Mind-Set

Consider two leaders who set out on a complex and difficult endeavor. Let's call them FM and GM, for reasons that will become clear in a minute. FM and GM are equally matched with respect to their abilities and motivation, yet these two leaders approach a task very differently. FM, a cyclone of unfocused energy, does not learn from feedback opportunities and appears frenetic, chaotic, and haphazard overall. GM is more organized and systematic and carefully considers all feedback. FM's counterproductive whirlwind is no match for GM's logical and calibrated approach, and GM easily outperforms FM by a significant margin. What can account for such radical differences between two individuals so clearly matched?

It turns out that FM and GM were prototypical participants in a very clever psychological experiment. FM refers to those who approached the task with a fixed mind-set—the assumption that their abilities were innate and not subject to change. GM refers to those who approached the task with a growth mind-set—the belief that their ability level was nothing more than a snapshot in time and eminently changeable as they continued to learn and develop.

Fixed Mind-Set: Recipe for Suboptimal Performance

Psychologist Carol Dweck argues that conditioning, beginning at a very young age, implicitly imposes a fixed mind-set. Virtually every adult has at some point told a youngster who did something well, "You are so smart!" According to Dweck, such messages build a belief that it is our inherent smartness that leads to good performance, not the effort that is exerted.

Through the associative processes of the automatic mind, these beliefs become forged with our identity. When things go well, we think it's because of how smart we are. When things don't turn out as we had hoped, we begin to doubt our ability. In other words, our mental model implicitly attributes performance—good or bad—to innate capabilities. We tend to think of capabilities such as problem solving, communication skills, and leadership as fixed and stable over time, hardwired by our genes. So, what is so wrong with that?

Quite a bit, actually. This mental model is a proven recipe for suboptimal performance over the long term. It becomes especially problematic when individuals with a fixed mind-set suffer a setback or make a mistake. They automatically associate their disappointing performance with an immutable deficit in abilities. This can diminish their confidence and spark an escalating spiral of negative emotion as they compare themselves unfavorably with others. More time spent in negative ideation means less time thinking about creative ways to improve performance. PR executive Rita Marshall started down this road when she was faced with not only the challenges of her new role but also a lack of confidence and support from her boss.

Surprisingly, research shows that a fixed mind-set can also be detrimental when things are going well. When people attribute their *good* performance to their innate ability, they tell themselves that effort and learning don't make much of a difference. Consequently, they select safer, less challenging routes where they can be assured of success, a pattern that further stagnates their growth.

Growth Mind-Set: Waking Up Smarter Every Day

A leader with a growth mind-set is consciously aware that ability is not innate and unchangeable but instead a malleable quality that can continuously be augmented through practice and persistence. In a growth mind-set, you pay conscious attention to cultivating abilities through continuous learning. You seek out new learning opportunities by pursuing challenging assignments instead of taking safer and easier routes. Kate Herzog, the eager learner from Ghana who transformed a little beachfront resort, embodied these characteristics as did Rita Marshall when she broke out of her negative pattern and began taking proactive steps to alter her situation.

Frank Gaudette, the chief financial officer (CFO) at Microsoft when I was there, also had a growth mind-set. Frank had a favorite expression: "I reserve the right to wake up smarter every day."

Unfortunately, Frank lost an untimely battle with cancer in the mid-1990s. Still his witty and humble expression serves as an eloquent reminder that every human being's abilities can change: you *can* get smarter; you *can* get better. Frank's words still echo in my mind and, I am sure, in the minds of everyone else who was privileged to know him.

There is compelling scientific evidence that a growth mind-set can significantly improve performance. In the experiment mentioned earlier, participants with a growth mind-set (GM) performed significantly better on a difficult managerial decision-making task than those whose mental models told them that their abilities were innate and fixed (FM). Participants with a growth mind-set were also more optimistic about their future performance, set higher personal goals, and used more-effective strategies than their colleagues.

Another fascinating finding of the study is that participants who carried a fixed mental model—that is, those who believed that their performance on the task was a reflection of their innate ability— actually had higher levels of activity than participants in the growth mind-set group. They were, however, more likely to spend time on nonproductive strategies rather than search for the effective strategies that would improve their performance.

Given that this finding is crucial to a deeper understanding of the differences between the two mind-sets, it may be helpful to take a closer look at the different strategies that participants used to complete the task. Those in the growth mind-set group productively used the feedback they received and systematically altered each of the variables in the task to understand and isolate its effect on the outcome. Tapping into their reflective mind in this way allowed them to deploy wiser strategies in the later stages as their knowledge of the task improved.

As noted, those in the fixed mind-set group actually exerted more energy. They altered even more variables in the simulation task, but did so in an undisciplined and unproductive manner. In essence their busyness resembled futile thrashing more than effective problem solving. Instead of incorporating negative feedback to improve performance, the energy in the fixed mind-set group turned inward, consumed by an escalating cycle of self-doubt that interfered with both learning and performance.

The following chart compares the characteristics of a fixed mind-set versus a growth mind-set.

A Fixed Mind-Set versus a Growth Mind-Set

	Fixed Mind-Set	Growth Mind-Set
Assumption about abilities	Implicit assumption that abilities are fixed and innate, not subject to change.	Conviction that abilities can improve over time with practice, persistence, and training.
Attribution of failure	See failure as a reflection of ability.	Failure inspires search for new ways to improve skills.
Performance during difficult tasks	When challenged, tend to compare themselves with others who are perceived as having greater abilities. During difficult tasks, strategies become disorganized and chaotic. They may try hard, but aren't thoughtful enough to create effective solutions.	During difficult tasks, strategies are systematic and goal directed. Make productive use of feedback to improve performance.
Attribution of success	Tendency to attribute success to innate ability.	Tendency to attribute success to the result of effort and hard work.
Choice of work assignments	Tendency to choose easy, unchallenging projects to avoid failure that might expose personal inadequacies.	Tendency to choose difficult and challenging assignments to grow skills.

Ultimately, Frank Gaudette's mantra is supported by hard scientific evidence. You *can* increase your capacity and capabilities each and every day—if you set your mind to doing so. Here's how.

Adopt a Growth Mind-Set through Reflection

The first step in adopting a growth mind-set is to pay attention to what's going on around you and give the reflective mind a mandate to take control. You can begin simply by elevating your awareness.

To get the most out of the following exercises, and others like them throughout the book, I suggest keeping a notebook, a place to jot down thoughts and responses to questions. The simple act of starting a leadership notebook is an affirmation of your commitment to adopt a new mind-set.

Customize your notebook to suit your preferences, or you can purchase one from my website at www.snyderleadership.com. You can jot down your thoughts on paper or in a digital file. If you think better visually, you can add sketches, charts, or other relevant images to your written thoughts. If you're more comfortable articulating your thoughts verbally rather than writing them down, you may decide to keep an audio journal.

Reflective Exercise: Tell Your Struggle Story

Writing or recording a specific struggle story of your own will help you better relate to and benefit from all the other exercises, stories, and practices woven throughout this book. Your story might be a struggle you are currently facing, or it may be a past struggle that you'd like to examine more deeply. Begin by writing about the experience as if you were telling a friend about it. Bring your story to life by describing the circumstances that led to the struggle, the relationships you had with the other people involved, your feelings about what happened, and any other colorful details that come to mind. If your story occurred in the past, record how the episode ended and what you learned from it. If you can't find the right words to explain something, take a short break, but be sure to come back to it.

Remind yourself that this exercise is an integral part of a valuable learning journey and that part of learning is stretching beyond your comfort zone. Taking the time and the energy to write down your struggle story is an important investment in your growth as a leader.

After you have written your struggle story, ask yourself the following questions:

- How do the three defining elements of leadership struggle— change, tension, being out of balance—apply to your story?

- What script or scripts did you follow?

Reflective Exercise: Recognize Adaptive Behaviors and Interfering Behaviors

Now, building on the struggle story that you've written, draw two columns in your notebook and label them "Adaptive Behaviors" and "Interfering Behaviors." In the first column, list the adaptive behaviors you see in yourself that contribute to your personal and professional growth and success; it could be those behaviors that helped you navigate through your struggle. There should be a lot of them! In the second column, list the behaviors that you think may be holding you back.

To give you an idea of what the format and the content might look like, on the following page is a sample chart for someone who was passed over for a promotion and is using the opportunity for some candid reflection.

After completing your chart, set aside some time for reflection. First focus on your adaptive behaviors. Allow yourself to feel good about the positive ways you live your life. Then move on to the other side of the ledger. How do the behaviors you listed interfere with your growth and success?

Sample Chart of Adaptive Behaviors and Interfering Behaviors

Adaptive Behaviors	Interfering Behaviors
▪ I am very creative. I am constantly coming up with out-of-the box ideas.	▪ I find myself procrastinating on important tasks and sometimes find it difficult to stay focused.
▪ I read a lot and stay up-to-date on industry developments and trends.	▪ Sometimes I can be irritable, moody, and impatient.
▪ I keep physically fit, exercise regularly, and watch my diet.	▪ I often find myself interrupting others when they are talking.
▪ I am close with my family and have many friends outside of work.	▪ I am too much of a loner at work. I haven't taken the time to build good working relationships with my colleagues.
▪ I am self-reflective, consider myself a lifelong learner, and continually work at self-improvement.	

Develop a Regular Practice of Reflection

Start a regular introspection practice by devoting at least 30 minutes a week for reflection and contemplation. Choose a time that feels good for you, perhaps on a Friday, Saturday, or Sunday. Ask yourself about your experiences over the past week. What happened? How did you feel?

If the experience was a positive one, ask yourself, *How did my efforts contribute to the outcome?* If the experience was unfavorable, ask yourself, *How can I improve my abilities so I will be more adept at handling such situations in the future?*

Pay particular attention to the times your automatic mind sends you contrary messages. For example, notice any thoughts you may have about comparing your abilities with those of others, or any thoughts casting doubts on your abilities. These thoughts, which are indicative of a fixed mind-set, carry with them latent assumptions that abilities are fixed and innate. When you recognize such a thought, tell your reflective mind to send you a wink and a smile. That way you'll know your reflective mind is starting to get stronger.

Refer to your two-column chart of adaptive and interfering behaviors. Can you think of anything to add to either column? Are there any interfering behaviors you can remove from the chart because they no longer define you?

After practicing this weekly reflective exercise for two or three months, review what you've written in your notebook and look for signs of the growth you've cultivated through your discipline and focus. Ask yourself: *How did I put my growth mind-set to work?* Be prepared to be amazed when you see how far you've come in such a short time.

GROUNDING PRACTICE
Become Resilient in the Face of Failure

My most intense personal struggle unfolded when I was 28. Five years earlier, after graduating from business school, I had set out for New York City to work at a large management-consulting firm. While I was employed there, a number of other job opportunities came my way, but none was as interesting as the call I got in January 1982 from an old friend, inviting me to join a startup company in Boston. My wife and I were fond of Boston, where I had attended business school, and we were excited to move back. We bought a lovely house, I enjoyed the challenge of my new job, and we were quite happy. Suddenly, in November, the startup collapsed. Just like that I was out of a job.

The economy was in a recession, and national unemployment was more than 10 percent. I was saddled with a 13 percent mortgage, and cash started gushing from my bank account. For the first time in my life, I went into a tailspin. My confidence plummeted, and the whole world seemed to be crashing down around me. It felt like a gigantic hole had been cut in my gut.

As I look back on that time, I now realize that my automatic mind had panicked and was filling that hole with fear-based thoughts and feelings as fast I could produce them. That hole in my gut became a whirlpool of negative energy, and my psyche was helplessly swirling around in the vortex, drowning in self-pity. I imagine that my reflective mind was calling out to me, trying to help, but hearing it in the midst of my panic would have been like trying to listen to a whisper in a windstorm.

I did not have the skills back then to methodically pull myself out of a nosedive. Today, if I feel the icy grip of fear on my shoulder, I know exactly what to do: I figuratively step back from the fear and instruct my reflective mind to call a time-out. But more on that in a moment. You're probably wondering how I managed to avoid a complete meltdown all those years ago.

At the time I didn't realize it was a coping mechanism, but whenever I was in my car I would play a Dan Fogelberg tape, *The Innocent Age*. The high-energy songs boosted my mood and offered me a veritable string of philosophical pearls. This may sound a bit silly, but one song, "Run for the Roses," seemed to speak directly to me. It was about a racehorse being groomed to run in the Kentucky Derby. The chorus urges the horse to "run for the roses as fast as you can," declaring,

> *It's the chance of a lifetime*
> *In a lifetime of chance*
> *And it's high time you joined*
> *In the dance.*

Hearing this song over and over again somehow gave me the stamina I needed to keep going, remaining in the dance when all I wanted to do was curl up into a ball and be alone.

As it turned out, that one thing—staying in the dance—made all the difference. Despite numerous setbacks, I stubbornly kept plowing ahead in my quest to find a new job. Ironically, it was during my unemployment struggle that Steve Jobs had unveiled the Lisa computer. Hearing of that presentation, I had been painfully aware of my own struggles, never dreaming that, despite Jobs's slick exterior, he was going through tremendous struggles of his own.

Two weeks later Bill Gates came to Boston to speak at Harvard Business School. I knew it was part of a recruiting trip for newly minted MBAs, and because I had graduated five years earlier technically I was not invited. Still I knew the drill, so I crashed the party. At the reception following Bill's talk, I walked up to him, introduced myself, and ultimately was the only person hired from the recruiting trip. In an instant I had gone from jobless and almost desperate to finding myself in a pivotal role at Microsoft: working to stabilize Microsoft's relationship with IBM. As it turns out, losing my job had been a blessing in disguise, creating the space for an even better opportunity that would launch my career into hyperdrive.

Staying in the Dance

In the midst of failure or adversity, you may feel, as I did, like curling up and surrendering. That of course is not an option. Summoning the courage and the inspiration to stay in the dance is mandatory.

Those who find strength through religious faith may be comforted by their belief that a trusted, intelligent force will lead them safely through their struggle. Others may persist out of sheer necessity, driven by a sense of duty to their family or organization. Still others lunge forward by dint of tenacity, simply refusing to accept the status quo. In my own struggle, I discovered that inspiration can be found in unlikely places, such as a song.

Finding what works for you is what's important. If you need to redefine the dance as you go along, so be it. My own dance was clear and well defined: finding a job. In some cases, however, staying in the same dance, or even trying to adapt it, may be futile. You may need to find a different dance altogether or to choreograph one of your own. No matter which path you take, the strategies offered in subsequent chapters will be helpful.

Learning New Dance Steps: The ABCs

Staying in the dance is not always enough, of course. Sometimes you have to learn some new dance steps. The first move to learn is how to slam on the brakes on your automatic mind so that it stops feeding you a constant barrage of negative thoughts and feelings, such as fear, anger, helplessness, and vindictiveness.

Once you understand how the automatic mind works, you can transcend this pattern of negativity by applying the ABCs of resilience: *adversity, beliefs,* and *consequences.*

The ABCs of Resilience

When you suffer adversity, your mind feverishly seeks to uncover the cause of it, interpret the meaning of it, and forecast its impact on your future. This sense-making process, which typically happens unconsciously, is tangled up with a set of implicit beliefs or assumptions that you may have never fully examined. Often these beliefs are maladaptive; they may send you veering off on a detour by conjuring memories of a past trauma or tapping into longstanding fears or stereotypes. Whatever the origin of these dysfunctional beliefs, their adversity-induced activation produces predictable consequences: feelings or behaviors that are themselves counterproductive.

Let's say you are working very hard on a project that you really believe in. Suddenly, your boss cancels the project and reassigns you to another task. Your disappointment may be exacerbated by an underlying belief like, *My boss hates me, treats me unfairly, and is just waiting to fire me.* Consequently, you might feel angry, hurt, powerless, vengeful, scared, or even trapped.

Normally, the path from adversity to consequences is so rapid that underlying beliefs never cross your mind. In other words, you go from A directly to C. You can alter this pattern by activating your reflective mind to explicitly examine your beliefs and consciously inserting healthier, more adaptive ones.

For example, instead of the belief that your boss treats you unfairly and is waiting to fire you, a more constructive set of beliefs might be: *My boss probably had good reason to make the decision she did. I would be better served by trying to understand her motivations and logic, taking care to be respectful of her authority as a leader and dignity as a person. Perhaps this new assignment will enable me to contribute more to the organization, potentially advancing my career.* Substituting this new belief structure would immediately lead to more-positive feelings and more-fruitful action.

Reflective Exercise: Practice the ABCs

Take a minute to reflect in your notebook about a cycle of escalating emotions or counterproductive behaviors you've experienced. Dig deeply to discover the underlying beliefs that impelled you to feel or act as you did. Now write down some alternative beliefs that are more adaptive. What consequences would these new beliefs have produced?

Now look at the material in your notebook generated from the earlier exercises in this book, examining them through the ABC framework. Do the ABCs give you more insight into understanding your long-held beliefs? Can you now begin substituting dysfunctional beliefs with more-adaptive ones? As you begin to build a new vocabulary of beliefs, strive to intentionally insert these healthier beliefs into your thought process. You will find that when you change your beliefs, you change your perspective, which changes your thinking, which changes your behavior, which changes everything.

Make Sense of a Chaotic World

What I need is perspective. . . . Otherwise you live
with your face squashed against a wall, everything
a huge foreground, of details, close-ups, hairs, the
weave of the bedsheet, the molecules of the face.

— Margaret Atwood, *The Handmaid's Tale*

Tension Points

"The world as it is," as the Struggle Lens suggests, is chaotic indeed. Such chaos might leave a leader feeling flustered, out of balance, and out of control. Seeking to discern the specific tensions underlying a challenging situation is a good next step toward managing through the complexity. With a better understanding of how these tensions work, you will gain a clearer perspective and make better choices.

Not only is change at the heart of leadership struggle, it is also a source of the emotional and physical tension a leader feels as a result of that struggle. Joe Dowling's story colorfully captures the multifaceted relationships among change, tension, and struggle. His cautionary tale also illustrates four tension points that grow out of struggle: tensions of tradition, tensions of aspiration, tensions of relationships, and tensions of identity.

Tensions of tradition and aspiration organize along the dimension of time, one looking to the past and having a historical connection and the other looking forward. Tensions of relationships have their locus in the outside world, where connections between and among people can either amplify or deflate the emotional energy within a system. Tensions of identity are found in your inner world: within your heart, mind, and soul.

Power Struggle

When in 1978 Joe Dowling landed the top job of artistic director at the Abbey Theatre, the National Theatre of Ireland, he made a big splash. At 28 he was the youngest artistic director in the theater's history. Little did he know that he was embarking on a chaotic odyssey that he would come to regard as perhaps the most difficult experience in his professional career. Yet at the same time, his tenure there would be pivotal in transforming him into the great leader he is today.

Dowling's vision for the Abbey and for himself as artistic director was thwarted by disagreements with the board of directors. Almost from the beginning, Dowling was at odds with the board, and the relationship only grew more contentious over time. When Dowling took over, the board of directors was very much hands-on. Stemming from a time when there was no professional management, the board made all the important decisions, including the selection of plays. Even though there were professional managers before Dowling, the board never seemed to let go. At least that was Dowling's perception.

Dowling brought a very different understanding of the respective roles of the board and its artistic director. He saw the artistic director as the CEO, who should command considerably more authority in the theater's management, including the selection of plays. Dowling was eager to steer the Abbey in this direction, which put him in direct conflict with the board.

After several years a compromise was reached that would give Dowling the authority he desired. But the accord "didn't go well" with some of the board members, who steadfastly believed that the board should remain actively involved in the management of the theater, especially the selection of plays.

Several years later the Abbey ran into financial difficulties. To save money, the board issued a directive that the theater could not employ any guest artists; only artists already on the payroll could be deployed for productions. Long-smoldering emotions erupted at that point. Dowling felt that by preempting him the board had stripped him of his authority, which he had fought hard to attain and preserve over many years.

Dowling confronted the board, but they would not back down, so he decided to take bold action. He abruptly and publicly resigned.

Tensions of Tradition

What fueled the tension between Dowling and the Abbey's board members? At the beginning of Dowling's tenure as artistic director, there were radical differences of opinion between them, resulting from different assumptions about the respective roles and responsibilities of the artistic director and the board.

Throughout its history until Dowling arrived, the Abbey's board had played an integral role in the management of the theater. Perhaps the board did not see as clearly as Dowling did the opportunities that professional management could afford. A great artistic director can bring a clarity of vision and focus that simply cannot be achieved by a committee. The artistic director is the master of blending experimentation with classics to tap into the soul of the theatergoing community. It is through this process of innovation and reinvention that a theater can distinguish itself over the long run.

At the Abbey, however, play selection was more than a matter of management and artistic vision. The board saw itself as a steward of a national institution, whose mission was, in Dowling's words, to "reflect back to a nation itself, through theater." Some board members were politically appointed and may have seen their role in play selection as an integral part of their stewardship. By wresting play selection authority away from the board, Dowling may have unintentionally sent a signal that he did not honor or respect the board's traditional role as stewards of the theatrical treasure chest of Ireland.

Despite the compromise that had been reached, tensions of differing traditions may not have been truly resolved, giving way to an uneasy relationship between Dowling and the board.

Tensions of tradition occur as leaders confront the implications of breaking with patterns from which they and others have become accustomed. In organizations these practices are generally rooted in previous adaptations; at some point in the past, they were most likely healthy and appropriate. These traditions form the basis of an organization's culture, and there is generally a widely held assumption that they are worth holding on to. New leaders often bring different assumptions, which may come into conflict with these established patterns and traditions, generating new tensions and struggles, as Dowling discovered.

Tensions of tradition can also arise when some new element is introduced to the environment, either as a surprise or as part of a long-term trend. In such a scenario, once-adaptive traditions and customs can become an albatross, holding an organization back and creating fresh tensions as a leader struggles to turn the ship.

Tensions of Relationships

In any organization, managing relationships is critical to getting things done. But even more importantly, relationships form the basis of connection from one human being to another that can bring fulfillment in everyday exchanges. In a healthy relationship, virtually every interaction generates positive energy. Even when there is a difference of opinion, respectful dialogue can build trust and foster mutual satisfaction. A healthy culture of creativity and collaboration helps the relationship withstand crises.

At the Abbey, the opposite seemed to be true. Interactions between Dowling and the board did not build positive energy and in many cases were an energy drain. Residual conflicts from unresolved differences in traditions may have contributed to the growing tension. As Dowling noted, "There was no doubt that the history of confrontation, which had gone on for seven or eight years on issues large and small, was a pattern that seemed to be escalating."

These tensions prevented Dowling and the board from building the type of respectful and trusting relationship that's needed to endure the stress a crisis can bring. This dynamic proved to be a fatal flaw in the relationship when the Abbey ran into financial difficulties.

Tensions of Aspiration

Tensions of aspiration are forward looking. They arise as an organization mobilizes around a dream or vision for the future. Sometimes these tensions bubble to the surface when different stakeholders bring different visions or values into proposed solutions or goals, as was the case at the Abbey Theatre. Sometimes they manifest when short-term incentive systems do not completely align with long-term organizational values. Sometimes the culprit is sheer ambition, as tensions manifest through the natural energy that is created when people with differing agendas work together on difficult endeavors in which more than one path appears viable.

At the Abbey tensions erupted as Dowling and the board clashed over the theater's financial problems. Entrenched in the hardened cement of competing priorities, their radically different approaches blocked them from arriving at an agreement in which artistic excellence and fiscal conservatism could peacefully coexist.

Implicitly, it is clear that the board aspired to find a solution that emphasized fiscal conservatism. Dowling, while recognizing the need for fiscal prudence, also saw the need to strive for artistic excellence. Had there been healthy relationships and an underlying level of trust, a dialogue could have occurred that included discussion and debate of different approaches. Perhaps, if this had taken place, a collaboratively generated solution would have emerged that appropriately balanced these two values and satisfied both Dowling and the board.

What actually happened was very different. Tensions escalated further until virtually all the energy and dialogue swirled around the issue of artistic director authority. Dowling may have been right; appropriately delineating boundaries of authority and responsibilities may have been important for the long-term health of the theater. In light of historical tensions, however, going all in on the issue at that precise time may have distracted attention away from finding a workable solution to the pressing financial problems.

Tensions of Identity

Tensions of identity can occur as leaders wrestle with issues surrounding their values, integrity, and authenticity. They may find it necessary to make difficult choices as circumstances pull them in multiple directions. The issues they contend with often have moral or ethical overtones.

Tensions of identity do not occur in every struggle episode, but when they do occur it is important to be mindful of them. These tensions are the ones that can shape a leader's character and have a lasting impact. It is in these defining moments that leaders grapple with the core issues of who they are and what they stand for.

Shakespeare wrote, "To thine own self be true." As leaders wrestle with tensions of identity, they gain deeper insight into the significance of these words. When they pause to reflect on new perceptions that arise while dealing with these tensions, they may ask, *What information, knowledge, or personal awareness am I missing?* or *What decision or action available to me is best aligned with my values?* Or, as the Struggle Lens suggests, *How do I choose among multiple important values? Which are the most important in this situation?*

In my work with leaders, I have seen tensions of identity play out along three broad outlines. In one scenario the tension is resolved as the leader comes to a new understanding of a situation and how to proceed effectively and with integrity. Sometimes a creative spark illuminates a fresh new alternative that had not previously been considered. Sometimes leaders are able to modify their role, behavior, or perceptions in ways that allow them to feel more autonomy and satisfaction with their work. As their adaptive energy guides them back into harmony with the circumstances at hand, the tension is resolved.

In the case of Rita Marshall, the PR leader, she found it difficult to lead with conviction and authenticity as she began to doubt her own credibility. This self-doubt created the tension that propelled her into action. Engaging her reflective mind, she reframed her perception of the situation and took responsibility for what she could control. A creative spark inspired her to seek professional accreditation and support. Through internal validation supported by external credentials, Marshall gained the confidence to move forward and excel in her new position. The tension was resolved, allowing her to work within an advertising model until the time was right to build her own organization.

In a second scenario, it is leaders' own self-concept and identity that undergoes a shift as they reinvent themselves and their leadership, altering it to fit changing circumstances. This scenario will play out in Sandy Jones's story in chapter 5 and in Captain Joe Kelly's story in chapter 6.

In the third scenario, self-concept remains steadfast but the leader concludes that the situation is no longer tenable and that any efforts to improve it would be futile. Abandoning the search for creative solutions, he or she plans an exit strategy.

Depending on the circumstances, all three scenarios can be equally valid, and each carries its own risks. In the first one, we run the risk of acquiescing to suboptimal conditions and forgoing the opportunities afforded by seeking a fresh start elsewhere. In the second we risk becoming a chameleon, changing at the whim of a situational need, with no core mooring. In the third scenario, we risk missing key opportunities when we close our mind to new possibilities. Of course, there is always the option of combining approaches: proceed down the first path to diffuse a volatile short-term situation while simultaneously pursuing new long-term opportunities.

Resolving tensions of identity is central to navigating through struggle; as you navigate through this book, you will be building a repertoire of strategies to help you do just that. In Dowling's case, tensions had escalated to such a level that he could see no viable solution other than to publicly confront the board through his resignation. In his mind the issue of his authority became a matter of principle. Dowling was concerned that staying on at the Abbey and accepting the board's terms would set a precedent and tie the hands of future artistic directors. "I saw it as an absolute matter of principle, and therefore I was going to stand under that principle come hell or high water," he said.

Dowling quotes a line from James Joyce's *A Portrait of the Artist as a Young Man*, which had become his mantra since age 15: "*Non serviam. . . .* I will not serve that in which I no longer believe." Dowling had lost faith in the stewardship of the Abbey's board. He could no longer serve at the Abbey while remaining true to himself.

As Dowling's story unfolds, the tensions both escalate and proliferate. All the while, he is experiencing increasingly intense emotions that throw him further off balance. In my interview with him, he told me, "There was a lot of anger, a lot of frustration. There was a constant strain, which led me into bad health. It was never rational."

Ultimately, Dowling reached the point of total exhaustion:

> I was exhausted from spending more time preparing for those meetings than I was rehearsing plays and putting plays on the stage. It became all about *How do I get around this particular board member,* or *What is the atmosphere at board meetings going to be like? Where is the acrimony going to come from?* And all of that eventually made me feel *I can't do this job any longer.*

I'm spending so much time worrying about whether or not I'm going to get this thing through the board or not through the board.

Dowling Epilogue: From "I" to "We"

Dowling's leadership at the Abbey had transformed the theater after many years of stagnation. He helped develop new playwrights and actors. He created a higher level of public interest and excitement. Furthermore, his articulation of the respective roles of the artistic director and the board was visionary and ultimately would be adopted at the Abbey.

Still, Dowling's departure was abrupt, confrontational, and very public. It put his entire career in peril and left him, his family, and even the directors with long-lasting scars. Yet it would also prove to be a fulcrum that would pave the way for significant growth down the road.

At the Abbey, Dowling treasured being part of a larger mission. As the National Theatre of Ireland, the Abbey played a much bigger role in Irish culture than a commercial theater could have. "In the Abbey there is a much bigger vision, and that has always attracted me—to be part of something that is bigger and more substantial than my own ambitions," he told me.

The connection to a larger mission would be something Dowling would miss during his 10 years in commercial theater after leaving the Abbey. Then, in 1995, Dowling was named artistic director of the Guthrie Theater, a Tony Award–winning nonprofit regional theater in Minneapolis that is world renowned for its artistic and cultural aspirations.

Dowling recalls an early interaction with then–Guthrie board chair Margaret Wurtele. There was some disagreement between Dowling and the Guthrie board, which to Dowling was reminiscent of what had occurred at the Abbey: "Margaret looked at me in sort of horror and said, 'You do know, of course, that everybody on the board wants you to succeed.'"

This and other similar interactions would trigger something profound within Dowling. It was here that he would make the leap from a brilliant artistic director to the extraordinary leader he is today, energies aligned and adaptive.

Dowling would come to understand that his confrontational style may have obscured a *blind spot*—something he was not aware of or did not recognize as a problem—that made his tenure at the Abbey unduly contentious and stressful. In retrospect, Dowling told me:

> I think that if I had sat down individually with each of those board members and actually explained my position more cogently and clearly—if I had actually developed a majority by persuasion and conversation as opposed to confrontation—I think I probably could have gotten through that period. That would have been a more mature leadership style than I had at the time. I think I was very disrespectful of some of the board members. I saw them as enemies rather than as colleagues who needed to be persuaded.

At the Guthrie, Dowling would reconcile a paradox in his leadership identity that may have been irreconcilable at the Abbey. On one hand, Dowling yearned to be part of a mission that was larger than his personal aspirations. On the other hand, he needed autonomy and freedom to shape the vision of the institution. The paradox is that to be part of a larger mission, he needed to make space for the visions of other stakeholders who yearned to be part of that larger mission, as well.

The supportive environment at the Guthrie, created by Margaret Wurtele and other board members, was a perfect place to resolve this paradox. In so doing Dowling has emerged as a remarkable leader. When I asked him to describe his current model of leadership, he told me, "It really is about being clear, both about one's own place in the order of things and honoring everybody else's place. I am not the only person who puts the theater on here by a long way. I know that in order to make sure that we are a fully functioning organization, I need to be very respectful of the different people and different positions."

In *True North* Bill George talks about a transformation from "I" to "we." "We" is that state in which an individual is mindful that leadership is a team sport. In addition to advancing one's own vision, one becomes inclusive and respectful of the visions of others as well. During Dowling's chaotic struggle at the Abbey, he had not yet learned that winning personal battles of power is not as lucrative as the win-win outcomes that evolve when people move from "I" to "we" and open up a larger space for creative collaboration. Ultimately, his struggle would lead him to a place where he achieved this learning, realized more of his full potential as a visionary artistic director, and yet was also part of a larger mission.

Those who know Dowling now see him as an extraordinary leader who has made his mark on the community. In 2006 under Dowling's leadership, the Guthrie built a new $125 million complex with three performance stages that has become a landmark. Dowling is already the longest-serving artistic director of the Guthrie and plans to spend the remainder of his career there.

GROUNDING PRACTICE

Draw Your Tension Map

Dowling's tumultuous tenure at the Abbey Theatre illustrates how easy it is to be thrown off balance during a struggle episode. When egos and expectations clash, emotions can overwhelm rationality. It's a leader's job to make some semblance of sense out of chaos. The first step is to gain a clear understanding of what's causing the underlying tension. With a clear grasp of these tension points, a leader can become centered and determine the best way to navigate through the tension.

The four tension points introduced in this chapter—tradition, aspiration, relationships, and identity—are shown graphically in the following figure.

On the horizontal axis are two tension points that are present during change and transformation. Tensions of tradition arise when

Leadership Tension Map

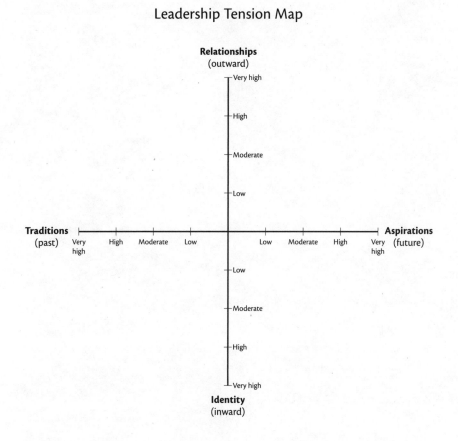

an organization confronts its past patterns, practices, and beliefs. Tensions of aspiration arise when a leader struggles to realize a different vision for the future.

On the vertical axis are two additional tension points, inwardly and outwardly focused. Tensions of relationships are outwardly focused and to a certain extent emerge from a climate of mistrust. Tensions of identity are inwardly focused and stem from an effort to express authentic and credible leadership capabilities.

The relative strength of each of the four tension points can be indicated by plotting them on the graph: the greater the tension, the farther from the center of the graph. For example, Dowling's tension map reveals a high level of tension at *all four* tension points.

Joe Dowling's Tension Points

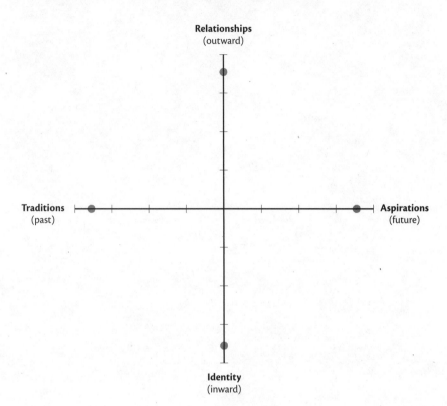

The map can then be completed by filling in the area bounded by the four plotted points. The directional arrows show whether each of the four tensions is increasing or decreasing. Dowling's tension map illustrates how his actions caused all four tension points to escalate.

Reflective Exercise: Draw Your Tension Map

Take a look at your own struggle story, the narrative you wrote about in the reflective exercise in chapter 3. Determine the relative strength of the four tension points as they relate to your story and plot them on a tension map of your own. Interpreting your tension map may give you insights into how to minimize or resolve each of the four tension points.

Joe Dowling's Tension Map

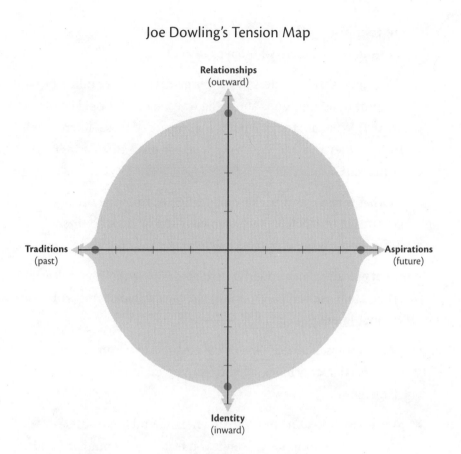

Below are some questions that can prompt your thinking. Explore the ones that seem most relevant by writing about them in your notebook. You may notice that some of the questions are worded to suggest alternative and perhaps more-adaptive beliefs that you can practice using the ABC model in chapter 3. In addition, visit my website to learn about additional tools for creating and navigating a tension map: www.snyderleadership.com.

Tensions of Tradition

■ What major changes are taking place in your industry or market? What impact do they have on your business? In what ways are your historical methods and customs holding you back from meeting the demands of today?

- Do different stakeholders in your organization have different customs or assumptions about the way business should be conducted? What are they? What is the impact of these differences? How do they relate to the changes taking place in your industry or market?

- In what ways is your background different from the backgrounds of others who appear in your story? How do these differences manifest in everyone involved?

- What are the values underlying these differences? Try to clearly articulate these values, especially the ones you disagree with, without judging them.

- In what ways, if any, are historical customs or assumptions by other participants blocking you from meeting your current challenges?

- What have you done to try to understand and honor these customs or assumptions, even if you feel they are outdated and dysfunctional? What aspects of these practices can be adaptively reformulated to meet the changing circumstances?

Tensions of Relationships

- If trust is a problem in your organization, how is mistrust interfering with getting your work done? Are you and your colleagues having courageous conversations around the table, or are you holding back during meetings and talking about important issues only in hushed tones in the hallway or at lunch with colleagues who agree with you? What issues do you need to be talking about with everyone involved?

■ In what ways are your relationships mutually fulfilling and respectful? In what ways are they an energy drain?

■ If you see any colleagues as adversaries, where is your anger and resentment coming from? Is this anger preventing you from seeing your colleagues as decent human beings who are as passionate about organizational values and goals as you are?

■ What behaviors are you exhibiting that exacerbate the situation and escalate the tension?

■ In what ways can you honor and respect the views of others without diminishing your own?

Tensions of Aspiration

■ How anxious do you feel about meeting your goals? What necessary skills, if any, are you lacking? If the goals are too ambitious or the path to meeting them unclear, what can you do to resolve these issues to the extent possible? What else is holding you back right now?

■ Do other stakeholders have differing visions of the "right" path the organization should take? If so, try to articulate the different points of view—and the values underlying them—of each of these colleagues. Try to explain these views and values in words that your colleagues would use, without judgment. How can you enter into a respectful dialogue with these colleagues while honoring and appreciating your differences?

■ In what ways, if any, are the explicitly stated goals of the organization inconsistent with its values?

■ In what ways, if any, do the organization's incentive systems not align with its short- and long-term goals and values?

■ In what ways, if any, are you focusing too much on your own agenda and not fully considering and integrating the goals and the agendas of others?

■ How can you respect aspects of everyone's values while staying true to the organization's mission?

Tensions of Identity

■ Do you have lingering self-doubts—times when you doubt that you have what it takes to be successful? What is the source of those doubts or fears?

■ In what ways does the "real you" come out when you are on the job? In what ways do you feel you need to be inauthentic to play your required role?

■ What, if any, ethical or moral issues are causing you tension at work?

■ How are your values consistent with the direction the organization is headed? How are they inconsistent?

■ Do you feel you have enough freedom to do your job? If not, under what constraints are you laboring?

■ What, if any, job-related yearnings have you not yet been able to realize?

■ In what ways, if any, are you feeling stress as you attempt to balance your job responsibilities and your commitments to your family and friends? In what ways are you dissatisfied with the way you are prioritizing your time?

■ What, if any, difficult decisions are you facing? What factors are making it difficult for you to decide what to do?

The Burnout Script

Recall the discussion of the burnout script in chapter 1. You read Steve Jobs's burnout story in chapter 2 and the narrative of Joe Dowling's burnout in this chapter.

At the beginning of a burnout script, life is good. Pre-burnout, leaders feel engaged and excited by their work, eager to make a difference, and optimistic that they can. But they soon find their goals stymied by obstacles they didn't expect and don't know how to overcome. They are thrown off balance when faced with the harsh reality that not everyone thinks as highly of their ideas as they do.

As the burnout script progresses, such leaders command less respect, as people don't seem to listen as carefully. They feel less and less in control and can feel disconnected and estranged. Their energy becomes drained and depleted. They can feel exhausted and spent; and, if they had the energy and the mental clarity to really pay attention, they would sense the exhaustion in others as well. They begin to question whether their efforts will make any headway and whether their aspirations will ever be realized.

Often such leaders blame others for their problems. They see themselves as in the right. When others don't agree with them, they feel angry or resentful, as if their dignity were under attack. If the struggle continues along these lines, the result is inevitable: such leaders either resign or are fired. Without gaining a sense of closure, they lug their emotional baggage with them wherever they go. Their agony remains raw, like a wound that is torn open anew by the slightest reminder of the ordeal.

If you have experienced the burnout script yourself, you may have cringed when you read these past few paragraphs. It may be too late to heal some of the damage inflicted during your struggle, but there is one wound that can be healed: your own.

Reflective Exercise: Heal an Old Wound

Think about a burnout script from your personal experience. Take a moment to reflect on it and record in your notebook the feelings that emerge as the details come flooding back. Give yourself the space to acknowledge that this happened to you but that it belongs to the past and is unchangeable. With the benefit of hindsight, and perhaps the growth and the wisdom that time can bestow, look for the lessons in the experience and learn what you can from it. If you ever again see the warning signs of approaching burnout, you will have the knowledge and the strategies to react more positively and productively.

The burnout script is more common than you may think. Many of the leaders I talked with shared a personal story that involved some degree of burnout. In every case, however, these extraordinary leaders found ways to reemerge stronger and wiser. Already, you have seen how Steve Jobs and Joe Dowling underwent remarkable metamorphoses, allowing them to flourish after their encounters with burnout because they learned from the experiences and grew as leaders.

If your current trajectory feels like a burnout script, there may still be the opportunity for a course correction—but only if you recognize what is happening with clarity and insight. Step back, engage your reflective mind, summon the wisdom of your adaptive energy, and consider all of your options before taking action. If you do not pause for reflection and simply persist in barreling ahead, tensions may continue to escalate until you reach a point of no return.

Of the six scripts that serve as undercurrents in leadership struggles, burnout is perhaps the most common culprit for throwing a leader off balance and off course. The next chapter offers two strategies for regaining that balance.

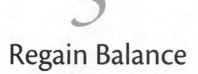

5

Regain Balance

It is the obvious which is so difficult to see most of the time. People say 'It's as plain as the nose on your face.' But how much of the nose on your face can you see, unless someone holds a mirror up to you?

— Isaac Asimov, *I, Robot*

JOE DOWLING'S TURBULENT TENURE AT IRELAND'S ABBEY THEATRE is an excellent case study in how struggle can throw a leader off balance. The more that Dowling's actions ratcheted up tensions, the further off balance he became and the more likely he was to act in ways that increased those tensions. Dowling's situation was notable because, while he found himself at odds with the board of directors, at least he and the board were sitting at the same table, albeit uncomfortably.

Many leaders do not have the same luxury. An organizational agenda—and the priorities and the goals that support it—is often set by others with whom the leader's relationship is distant at best. Depending on the culture and the hierarchy, power differentials may interfere with meaningful dialogue. In some cases it may appear that goals are set by a corporate machine that is detached, uncaring, and unaware of the "facts on the ground."

Sandy Jones's encounter with a "corporate machine" was nearly her undoing. A graduate of a prestigious business school, Jones found her passion in retailing. A quick study in climbing the corporate ladder, she rose to the level of senior vice president of merchandising with a large department store retailer while still in her thirties. She had survived, and even thrived, through many changes as the retail industry began consolidating in the early 2000s. She was well along the road to reaching her dream of becoming chief merchant of a major retailer.

When her company was put up for sale, she dutifully, and perhaps even zestfully, prepared her team to weather the transition. Yes, there were new leadership styles and personalities to adapt to, new decision-chain logistics to consider, and new organizational standards to contend with, yet somehow Jones found the strength to authentically lead her team through it all. She understood that change was part of a systematic shift that was necessary for the retail industry's long-term survival.

Just as Jones was beginning to find her footing with the new organization, the parent company that had acquired her company was bought by another major department store chain—let's call it Lasman's—in a huge department store consolidation play. Suddenly, the strategies that had worked for her for so many years were no longer effective, which naturally threw her off balance. Jones was about to enter the most intense struggle of her professional career, which would ultimately alter her identity as a leader and put her career on a completely new trajectory. But first she would have to confront her worst fears and live through her worst nightmare.

Adaptive Skills

Over the years, Jones had diligently cultivated the skills necessary to navigate the numerous challenges she faced. For instance, her job in retailing required her to develop the proficiency to dive deeply into data. While Jones did not see herself as a numbers person, she soon acquired an intuitive sense for spotting trends and forecasting. When faced with a new challenge, she would probe and ask questions, teasing apart the complexity until she uncovered the root cause of the problem.

She also had an excellent support network. She had a solid relationship with her husband, and she had a twin sister with whom she could share everything. She had her running buddies, who would

gather for coffee after their weekly runs. She also enjoyed supportive relationships at work. The executive team was very cohesive and
offered mutual encouragement. "There were 10 of us on the executive
team, and every week we went out for drinks and shared stories," she
told me.

Jones also learned how to keep her mind clear and tap into positive energy. "Even just walking through the halls where my team was
sitting, if I was in a good place mentally, it felt like my energy helped
elevate everyone's mood," she said.

A marathon runner, she had learned how to discipline her mind
and body to keep herself in balance. She talked about preparing for
particularly stressful meetings where she knew her leadership would
be tested: "I would not only do Pilates, I would also probably run 8
miles," she said. "I would get myself totally pumped up so I could be
as energetic and authentic as possible." In addition to exercising and
spending time in nature, Jones developed a meditation and mindfulness practice to gain added clarity. Her daily routine was her anchor
for whatever winds would blow her way.

Not only had Jones developed great skills for guiding her mind
and body through stressful experiences, she had also become adept at
channeling this centering energy into strategies for leading her team.
With each change she experienced, she gained clarity about how to
successfully navigate the next one. A visual thinker, she drew a big
starburst on the wall of her office, explaining to her team:

> A year from now, we are going to be feeling good. We are going to
> have mastered all of this. And we are going to take it in chunks.
> Here are the milestones we are going to achieve. It will be up to
> you to figure out how to accomplish them.

> Every month we got together and inevitably things changed, but
> I always brought them back to that visual of the starburst. I said,
> "This is what happened, this is what we did, and that's how it
> changes these particular things." And we started moving through it.

Then Lasman's took over and the changes, the stress, and the struggle rose to a whole new level of intensity. Many of Jones's well-developed adaptive strategies were no longer relevant, and she soon began to feel more out of balance than she ever had before.

Mission Impossible

When Lasman's took over, the entire management team was summoned to headquarters, where they were given two directives. First they were told to change their merchandise assortment by 40 percent—in other words, replace 40 percent of all the items in the store with new items. Second, they learned that in eight months, when the Lasman's sign went up, Lasman's would be expecting a double-digit increase in sales.

The practicalities of the first directive flew against everything that Jones had been taught as a retailer. It meant that within three weeks, the merchandising team had to fly to New York and buy products "that we didn't know anything about."

The second directive seemed even more unrealistic. Not only did the merchandising team need to change nearly half the assortment in the store but, magically, they somehow had to produce a double-digit increase in sales in a chain where sales had declined in each of the previous five years. All of Jones's experience told her that this was beyond impossible; it was unimaginable.

The interpersonal style of the new Lasman's management team added yet another stressor:

> There was one presentation I will never forget. I worked really hard. They asked us to be very strategic, so I talked about what the strategy was going to be and the key initiatives. And one of Lasman's senior leaders stopped me in the middle of talking and said, "You know, I don't know how people even understand you or follow you when you talk."

Here I was, talking the way I always talk, the way that had gotten me great feedback through my whole leadership career. And the person in charge just stops me 15 minutes into my presentation and tells me in front of everybody, "I don't understand what you're saying," in a really arrogant and derogatory sort of way. All of a sudden, everyone in the room is looking at you like you are an absolute idiot.

Jones's story is a classic mission-impossible script. Lasman's corporate team not only set goals unilaterally that were impossible to reach but they simultaneously torpedoed any chance of achieving them by mandating a dramatic and rapid shift in assortment. Add a prickly interpersonal climate to the mix, and the inevitable result is a system engulfed in tension.

The following factors exacerbated the stress and the tension:

- Jones had established a tradition of making decisions with data and a fairly constant customer base, whereas in the current situation historical data was simply not available for the new assortment, nor was it clear how loyal customers would react (tensions of tradition).

- The Lasman's process brought buyers from other divisions together. These meetings were often combative and competitive, further eroding trust (tensions of relationships). This was in stark contrast to the collaborative spirit that Jones was accustomed to (tensions of tradition).

- Most of Jones's divisional peers were jumping ship and being replaced with Lasman's people, which further eroded comfort and trust (tensions of relationships).

- When the Lasman's sign finally went up, sales didn't go up by double digits as corporate had instructed. Instead they went *down* significantly. This precipitous slide raised additional questions as to whether the company was headed in the right direction (tensions of aspiration).

As all these factors coalesced, the impact began eroding Jones's confidence and core identity as a leader. She expressed her feelings with these observations:

- "It just felt very unsafe, like I didn't have an impact."

- "I wanted to be genuine and authentic but just did not know how."

- "I felt a loss of courage."

- "I could feel myself not quite knowing what to do much of the time, and I hadn't ever felt like that before. I knew there were some big decisions being made, and I could see what was going on, but there was no forum to talk about it."

- "I started to doubt myself: *I am not the merchant I thought I was. Do I really know what I'm doing?*"

For the first time in her life, Jones began to doubt her ability to deal with and overcome whatever adversity came her way. Not only did her lifelong ambition of becoming a chief merchant now seem unreachable but she began to fear she might even lose her job. Given that she was the sole breadwinner in her family—her husband had given up his job to help raise their children—losing her job would mean potentially losing everything: their house, their lifestyle, their future. Jones began to feel that she had failed herself and her family.

Despite the tsunami of emotion, intellectually Jones could fathom how Lasman's strategy made sense, at least over the long term. She could see the logic of industry consolidation and the resulting advantages of the increased buying power of a combined company. But this long-term light of reason shone dimly compared with the glare of her short-term struggle. Her visceral reactions to Lasman's unreasonable demands and callous management style were all the encouragement her automatic mind needed to taunt her with thoughts of failure in her most vulnerable moments. Only in retrospect would she be able to integrate all of this into a consistent worldview.

After Your Worst Nightmare, Rethinking Your Vision

Three years after the acquisition, Lasman's announced it would close down the divisional buying operation and Jones learned that she would soon lose her job. Her worst fears were realized. After absorbing the initial shock of that blow, something surprising happened: "That's when I felt all the freedom in the world," she said.

Jones's last three months with Lasman's were actually the highlight of her leadership career. Like a circle inexorably completing itself, all the strategies she had put in place years earlier became relevant once more. Once she had merchandising data to work with again, she was able to make better decisions. And by this time, all the economies of scale that had been only abstract concepts had materialized. With the scale of the combined companies working in their favor, the monolithic Lasman's was able to achieve the buying power and the cost advantages that had been beyond the reach of Jones's previous employer.

This was the glimmer of light that had inspired Jones back when Lasman's had first acquired the stores, but the fog of intense stress and tension had blotted out most of that light. By the time she started her last three months on the job, the fog had lifted and the light was shining brightly. In fact, business was so good that Jones's team beat their goals and earned a bonus that benefited not only her immediate team but also the entire company.

Reflecting on her experience, Jones realized that the self-doubt that had plagued her was unwarranted; she had taken the right path far more often than she had stumbled. She saw that in times of struggle, all she needed to do was trust in the process of adaptive action and the answers would come.

During my conversation with her, Jones recalled with some irony how she taught new buyers the basic "facts" of the business. She would tell them that, typically, it takes three years to turn around a business. Her judgment turned out to be spot on. That is exactly how long it took for everything to jell after the Lasman's acquisition.

After losing her job, Jones noticed that her career aspirations had evolved. She interviewed with other large retailers but decided not to accept any offers. Instead, through the help of personality tests, counseling, and meeting with her pastor, she began to reimagine her life's vision.

> I had taken tests that affirmed that I am very enterprising, but they also revealed that I am very service minded. My counselor at the time said, "This is really unusual. Usually, I don't see a very high enterprising drive combined with a very high service drive." That got me thinking because my twin sister is a special education teacher, and that's what also popped up: my profile is most similar to special education teachers.
>
> Soon after, while having lunch with my pastor, she said, "It's so curious that you keep on talking about these two sides of yourself." And she said, "Sandy, be one." It was like a thunderbolt moment for me. I am not just a merchant. I am me. I am a unique person with a unique point of view.

This epiphany moved Jones in a surprising new direction. She became interested in the developing field of holistic well-being. She sought out a university center that could give her the credentials to be a wellness counselor, and she started taking courses.

Armed with this new vision, Jones forged her own unique path. Her life's mission has changed. Instead of envisioning herself as the chief merchant of a large retailer, she sees herself as someone whose job it is to teach people how to improve their lives through well-being practices. She not only altered her job and her profession but connected them to her passion and her purpose, as well as to a larger mission. Like Joe Dowling and Steve Jobs, Jones found great comfort and strength through fidelity to a higher purpose.

Next are two practices that encompass the wisdom of Sandy Jones and other great leaders. The first practice will help you turn inward, focusing on how to remain centered, both spiritually and emotionally. The next practice will guide you in connecting with others to strengthen the nurturing relationships that are essential for healthy living during stressful times.

GROUNDING PRACTICE

Center Your Mind, Body, and Spirit

All leaders need some way to anchor and balance themselves in times of turbulence when forces beyond their control begin swirling around them with chaotic intensity. The leaders I talked to use a variety of practices to remain centered and grounded. Some focus on diet and exercise. Some seek to connect with something greater than themselves, either through organized religion or a more secular spiritual connection. Some find peace and tranquility by deeply connecting with nature. Others seek calmness and clarity through journaling. Many create their own unique blend of these practices and others.

One particular practice that emerged through my interviews, however, seems to function on a higher plane, transcending these other more traditional approaches. This is the practice of mindfulness.

The term *mindfulness* means different things to different people, so I will be specific about which approaches and techniques fall under the rubric of mindfulness for purposes of this book. The central focus is awareness. Mindfulness practices teach us to become more aware and more fully present while remaining peaceful within, even as chaos rages all around. In his book *Wherever You Go, There You Are: Mindfulness Meditation in Everyday Life,* Jon Kabat-Zinn writes:

> In essence, mindfulness is about wakefulness. Our minds are such that we are often more asleep than awake to the unique beauty and possibilities of each present moment as it unfolds. While it is in the nature of our mind to go on automatic pilot and lose touch with the only time we actually have to live, to grow, to feel, to love, to learn, to give shape to things, to heal, our mind also holds the deep innate capacity to help us awaken to our moments and use them to advantage for ourselves, for others, and for the world we inhabit.

So much of our time is spent *doing* things: creating action plans, conceiving strategies, anticipating obstacles, running meetings, planning for the future. Through mindfulness our focus turns to *being,* as in being fully present in the moment—fully awake, fully aware, and fully attentive.

Through the practice of mindfulness, we learn to objectively observe ourselves during stressful situations—as if both experiencing the situation and simultaneously watching ourselves from the balcony. The simple reflective act of naming our emotions as we experience them grants us a new power to more intentionally choose how we respond. Here is how Sandy Jones described her inner experience during a particularly uncomfortable meeting immediately after her company was acquired for the first time.

> The first time our new president had a meeting with us, it lasted eight hours. There was no agenda. There was no respect for the fact that it was 8:00 at night. And my body literally felt the discomfort. It was telling me, "This hurts." I would let myself feel that, but at the same time I would be watching myself feel it. My body would be talking to me, but I would also be thinking, *You are really feeling upset; you are feeling this fear.* I would let it happen and feel it but just realize it was part of the whole process.

Consider the following observation, which author Stephen Covey has credited with inspiring his life and work: "Between stimulus and response there is a space. In that space lies our freedom and our power to choose our response. In our response lies our growth and our happiness."

The practice of mindfulness trains us to maintain awareness of the space between our thoughts, short-circuiting the knee-jerk reactions of the automatic mind and engaging the reflective mind in creative new ways. As the automatic mind cedes authority to the reflective mind, the speed of life slows down, allowing us to consciously choose more-thoughtful responses to difficult and challenging situations.

Before meeting Sandy Jones, I had dabbled in the practice of meditation. But hearing Jones's vivid account of how she used mindfulness to anchor and steady herself, I became inspired to learn more. I took a course on Mindfulness Based Stress Reduction (MBSR) at the University of Minnesota's Center for Spirituality and Healing. The course is based on research by Jon Kabat-Zinn and features a combination of modalities such as meditation, yoga, and qigong, an ancient Chinese movement practice.

Also included are exercises like mindful eating and mindful walking, which teach students how to become fully present while doing activities that they normally take for granted. For example, mindfully eating an orange involves thinking about the process that brought that particular orange to you, appreciating the look and the feel of its shape and texture, savoring its nuanced flavors, and being aware of your own chewing, swallowing, and digesting of the orange.

Meditation is a cornerstone of the practice of mindfulness. When I meditate, which I try to do for at least eight minutes every day, I arrive at a state of inner serenity and calm. Everything slows down, and it feels like I have stepped off the treadmill of time. I am completely in the present moment—peaceful and relaxed.

In his book *Leadership from the Inside Out,* Kevin Cashman, a veteran practitioner of Transcendental Meditation, describes the meditative experience in this way:

> Like flashes of intuitive insight, awareness of Being, peace, spirit, or whatever we may wish to call it, comes to us in a quiet moment. It appears in the silence between our thoughts—the space between the problems and analysis. As we go within, the power of thought is greater. Just as atomic levels are more powerful than molecular levels, our deeper levels of thought have more energy and power. The third law of thermodynamics elucidates this natural flow of energy and power: As activity decreases, order increases. As the mind settles down, it becomes more orderly, more able to comprehend and to handle difficult challenges. As a result, we are able to go beyond the individual issues, combine seemingly unrelated variables, and come up with new solutions or perspectives.

The practice of mindfulness has already entered the mainstream conversation about leadership. In Western culture, which has long raised a collective eyebrow about such matters, people are benefiting from yoga, tai chi, qigong, and other meditative practices not only in the privacy of their homes or in scheduled classes but outdoors on university and corporate campuses as well as in other public spaces. Meditation rooms are springing up next to boardrooms at a brisk pace. Former Medtronic CEO and author Bill George, who has been practicing mindfulness meditation for more than 35 years, told me:

> I have a regular practice of meditation. I meditate two times a day for 20 minutes. I've done that since 1975. I meditate at the beginning of the day and at the end of the day, especially when the stress level is high. I also meditate every time I'm on an airplane. That 20 minutes after the doors close and we pull away from the gate until we take off is a perfect time to clear my mind.
>
> My personality is to be constantly busy. I have a lot of balls up in the air, and there are many things left incomplete—incomplete

interactions, loose ends. Meditation helps me get centered and focused on what's important. It's a way of cleaning all the clutter from my mind, like taking a shower.

I asked Bill about the time commitment a regular meditation practice requires. After all, people are so busy nowadays that 40 minutes a day for meditating sounds like an unimaginable luxury. Here's what Bill told me:

I get a lot of creative ideas when I meditate—when I am writing articles or teaching a class, things like what is a good opening question to start the class. When I was at Medtronic, I would have to sort through a number of difficult issues. Meditation would help me gain clarity.

I get a lot of energy when I meditate. Before I started meditating, I would feel that by 9 p.m. I was losing energy. When I meditate at 7 p.m., I find that I have energy to go until midnight.

Bill told me about a conversation he had with the Dalai Lama. Bill had asked His Holiness how he suggests we go about developing compassionate and authentic leaders. "The Dalai Lama replied that consistent practices are very important in leadership. Meditation is one of those practices. Jogging, exercise, and journaling are other possible practices, as is participating in a small group."

There is now compelling scientific evidence that mindfulness practices actually change brain functioning, essentially reprogramming the brain. Scientists scanned differences in the brain activity of individuals who participated in the eight-week MBSR training and compared them with a comparably matched control group. They found significantly more left-side prefrontal activation, the portion of the brain responsible for positive outlook and resilience. What's especially noteworthy is that these improvements continued to grow in the two months after the course ended. Also, those who went through the training reported significant reductions in anxiety symptoms.

Even more intriguing is the mind/body connection. Both groups were administered a standard flu vaccine. Those who received MBSR training produced more antibodies after receiving the vaccine, suggesting that meditation actually boosts the functioning of the human immune system.

Mindfulness research also indicates improved adaptation to stressful new assignments. A recent study showed that US Army trainees who received MBSR training showed greater resiliency prior to entering combat.

The science of how meditation affects brain processes is still in its infancy, but it is already clear that the brain is remarkably more alterable than scientists once thought. According to Richard Davidson, the researcher who pioneered the study of the impact of meditation on brain processes, "We all have habitual ways of responding to emotional challenges, and these habits are complicated products of genetics and experience. Mindfulness training alters these habits by making it more likely that one neuronal pathway rather than another will be used."

As my own practice continues to blossom, I have come to equate mindfulness to installing a new, enhanced operating system for the brain. Think of it as OS Brain 2.0. Lots of great features and benefits come standard: greater creativity, higher energy, more-thorough and proactive reflective processing, and greater happiness and sense of well-being.

What's more, the practice of mindfulness has a cascading effect, proliferating into many aspects of our lives. In his new book *The Power of Habit*, Charles Duhigg refers to this type of phenomenon as a "keystone habit." According to Duhigg, keystone habits create initial shifts that start "chain reactions," allowing other good habits to take hold.

If you'd like to learn more about mindfulness and explore how it can improve your leadership effectiveness, you can find some helpful resources on my website at www.snyderleadership.com. You'll find links to my favorite online meditations as well as some that were developed specifically to complement the material in this book. I hope these meditations help you embark on a path that is as fulfilling and joyous as mine has been.

Mindfulness is not the only effective centering practice. There are many practices you can use to ground yourself, such as walking in nature, deep prayer, listening to or playing music, painting, journaling or other forms of writing, working in a garden, sitting by water, and even swimming or running or other forms of exercise. There are probably as many different centering activities as there are people who engage in them. You will know that you have found the practice or practices that work for you when regular practice of them brings you renewed vitality and a jubilant sense of well-being.

GROUNDING PRACTICE

Find the Support You Need

The previous section introduced you to practices and tools for centering and grounding that guide you to turn your mind inward, creating a higher state of consciousness, inner serenity, and peace. In this section your focus is directed outward so that you can develop relationships and support systems to connect with others, seek their guidance, learn from their experiences, and receive valuable feedback. All the while you will be receiving the nurturing energy—and perhaps a healthy dose of tough love—that's inherent in supportive relationships.

Some organizations invest considerable resources in fostering a climate and a culture in which employees can thrive. They encourage teamwork and collaboration and implement formal and informal programs for developing leaders. One such organization is General Mills, which is consistently ranked among the best companies in the world for leadership development. Not surprisingly, General Mills is also ranked among the best companies to work for.

Marc Belton, executive vice president of global strategy, growth, and marketing innovation, told me that when he was facing some particularly thorny career challenges, he requested to work with an executive coach: "I worked with a coach for about a year so that I could get feedback from others, gain an external assessment, and clarify my personal mission and the things I wanted to do in the future."

At first the feedback wasn't easy to take, but Belton realized that "the feedback they were giving you wasn't because they didn't think you were good; they were doing it because they care about you and they're trying to give you things that will help you get better. So let's get to work on it. Let's move to the next level. Let's grow."

I asked Belton how the General Mills mission of "Nourishing Lives" connected with its strategy of developing leaders. He told me that the concept was originally intended as a corporate brand mission and that he was surprised "how much more holistic and robust it was than we thought it would be when we first started." It seemed to apply to all aspects of the company's business: "You nourish employees by developing them. You give them skills. And you hopefully let them fulfill their dreams by growing into the people they want to become."

If you work for a company like General Mills, you are fortunate. If your organization does not offer a supportive climate, you will need to be more resourceful, like PR executive Rita Marshall. She could not rely on any support within the company so she sought it externally, proactively creating her own support network in the process.

There are many ways to create your support system. Many people turn first to family and close friends. It is genuinely amazing how active, generous listening, or even just a well-timed hug, can help someone heal from the pain they feel in their life.

Often, however, family and friends cannot offer the quality of advice you need to cope with a difficult work situation. Then it is time to venture outside your existing network and proactively connect with people who can offer sound practical advice and guidance as well as support and encouragement. Mentors and coaches can fill this role as can peer support. Industry and trade associations are a popular way to connect with peers as are gender-specific groups. Some organizations, like Vistage, offer a combination of mentoring, coaching, and peer support.

One emerging approach for peer support is True North Groups, championed by Bill George and Doug Baker. True North Groups meet on a regular basis and offer a safe, trusting environment where members can open up, tell their stories, and express their fears and vulnerabilities. True North Groups foster intimacy and connection, qualities that rarely occur naturally in this transactional, fast-paced world. If the composition of a True North Group offers the right blend of expertise and experience, the group can provide advice and counsel and also serve as a sounding board.

In their book *True North Groups: A Powerful Path to Personal and Leadership Development*, George and Baker outline a process for choosing members, creating the right climate, structuring the appropriate agenda, and navigating through the pitfalls of group dynamics.

Reflective Exercise: Find Support from Others

Now it's time for you to craft your own strategy for finding the support you need. First write down all the people you can rely on for support. Many people find that if they put enough thought into it, the list will be far longer than they expected.

Now make a list of your needs for support. Don't just think of your current needs, no matter how important they may be. Think also of what your long-term needs may be as you develop and grow in your career. Think of the types of people you need who can guide, advise, and inspire you on your journey.

Next place your two lists side by side and match up your needs with the people in your support network. There may be short- or long-term gaps that can't be filled within your current network. It is these gaps that are most important. Here lie the opportunities for you to build your support network—providing for not only your current needs but also your long-term needs as you continue to grow and develop as a leader.

If you did not identify at least five new people to be on your long-term support team, you are not thinking hard enough about this issue. Remember, an integral part of the art of struggle is breaking out of old patterns and creating new habits to channel your energies in adaptive ways. Creating a community of people whom you can connect and bond with and from whom you can seek advice and feedback is a great way to get started.

Remember that connection is a two-way street: be sure to take into account how the other person is benefiting from your relationship; it then stands a far better chance of developing into a long-term, mutually fulfilling and enriching relationship.

Through my six-month employment crisis that ended with my landing at Microsoft, I learned firsthand the importance of supportive relationships. I was blessed to be on the receiving end of an outpouring of love and comfort from not only my wife Sherry but numerous good friends as well. Enduring the stress of that struggle was a small price to pay for the deeper bonds of love and friendship—and the stronger, more enriching sense of community—that grew out of it. Over the years my understanding of and appreciation for the nature of these vital connections has only deepened. I now see clearly that, through giving and receiving nurturance, we tap into one of the most fundamental of human yearnings: the deeply sacred and intimate experience of reaching out and touching another soul.

Part II

Exploring New Pathways

EXPLORING PRACTICES

Reimagine the Situation to Discover a New Creative Path

Reinvent Yourself

Overcome Your Blind Spots

Heal Yourself from Conflict

Envision the Common Ground

Write or Revise Your Personal Vision Statement

Recommit, Pivot, or Leap

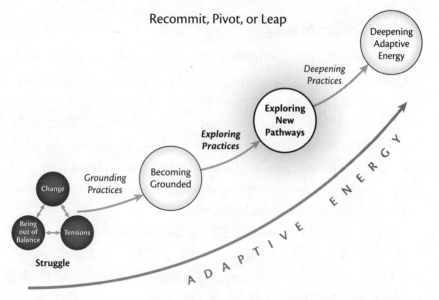

Navigate Tensions

Got to be the worst place in the world, inside a oven.
You in here, you either cleaning or you getting cooked.

— Kathryn Stockett, *The Help*

SANDY JONES, WHO HAD DREAMED OF BECOMING A CHIEF MERCHANT for a major retailer, emerged from her struggle to find herself on a different path that promised greater meaning and fulfillment. That was a very different struggle trajectory than the one followed by Kathee Tesija, who actually *did* become the chief merchant of one of the largest retailers in the world, Target Corporation.

Kathee Tesija's Struggle

Tesija became Target's top merchant in May 2008, just as Target, a $70 billion retailer, was noticing early signs of a softening market. Those warning signals foreshadowed the most precipitous business downturn that Tesija would experience in her 25 years at Target.

In her new role, Tesija became responsible for envisioning solutions that fulfill their guests' (Target's term for customers) changing needs. Tesija told me, "We work hard at understanding what they want before they can articulate what they want."

As the economy worsened during the summer and early fall of 2008, Tesija was faced with three challenges. The first was to understand and then address radical changes in the marketplace as unemployment climbed and people moved from ratcheting up their credit card balances to living within their means. "It was a very volatile time,"

Tesija noted. "We needed to understand what was happening with our guests very deeply, not just on the surface. Making the needed changes and adjustments was very complicated for a company the size of Target. Everything was so interdependent. Our model is based on sales growth, not on sales loss."

Her second challenge was managing through the short-term crisis while simultaneously executing the company's long-term strategic plan. Without neglecting the pressures of the moment, she needed to co-create and implement the new and innovative ideas that would be Target's pipeline for the future. At the time of the downturn, Tesija's team was involved in the pilot and the rollout of a new store prototype designed to make Target's stores more desirable and efficient for their guests. Much testing and time were required to ensure that these new ideas, the hallmark of Target's long-term innovation strategy, were carried out correctly. The new store prototype would have massive ripple effects, affecting not only store layout but also long-term vendor relationships and profitability models as well as the very expression of the Target brand.

Tesija's third challenge was to come up to speed in a new leadership role that involved learning to lead a larger team with more financial responsibility. She also needed to quickly familiarize herself with areas of the company that she had not previously managed.

Tesija approached these dilemmas with a mixture of emotions. On one hand she found the experience "frightening." With Target's reputation and so many people's livelihoods on the line, she felt "the weight of the world" on her shoulders. But she also described the challenge as "thrilling," "exhilarating," and "pretty darn exciting."

In the following analysis of Tesija's struggle, you will see that she was well prepared to meet her challenges. She was a seasoned executive whose star had shone brightly at Target for many years. You will see how she used creativity, innovation, and leadership to mitigate daily tensions and navigate successfully through the crisis. You will also see that she benefited from organizational support; aspects of the Target culture served to moderate tensions, creating an optimal environment in which she could thrive and grow.

Navigating through Tensions of Tradition and Aspiration

It is easy to imagine how a variety of traditions can become culturally ingrained in a $70 billion behemoth like Target. It is just as easy to imagine that considerable tension might surface as Tesija attempted to break with tradition and implement the changes necessary to adjust to a rapidly changing environment.

Fortunately, Tesija possessed the leadership skills to ease the tensions that otherwise may have engulfed her team. She widely communicated the need for change, including the need to "look under every rock." Her leadership set an organizational expectation that change could and should be radical and pervasive in times of turmoil. By embracing and communicating the need for change, Tesija created a climate that assuaged the fears that people typically have when they are jolted from previously comfortable patterns. She also enlisted willing team members as change agents, which gave others the opportunity to take ownership of the change process, as well.

Target's culture, which champions innovation and change, was a key asset in alleviating tensions of tradition. One of the company's core values is "fast, fun, and friendly," which it expresses thusly: "Every team member is encouraged to innovate, contribute ideas and discover solutions as an important part of a world-class team."

The two primary factors behind the tensions of aspiration that beset Tesija's team were beyond their control. The first was uncertainty. Despite extensive research, it was impossible to get a good grip on reality because reality was constantly shifting. Uncertainty of course breeds fear, and many members of Tesija's team were living through their first economic downturn. Tesija worked to ease their fear through a continuous flow of candid communication and by serving as "the steady hand guiding the ship—connecting them to the strategy, reassuring them, and helping them understand."

The second source of aspirational tension was time. There simply were not enough hours in the day to get everything done, especially considering that Tesija's group had previously committed to rolling out a new store prototype just before the financial crisis hit. Managing that piece of the business alone would require an inordinate amount of time in the best of circumstances; with the marketplace in upheaval, keeping the rollout on schedule seemed unreasonable and unattainable. To complicate matters further, previously unplanned research projects needed to be hastily designed and implemented to take the pulse of a marketplace in constant flux. Such surveys, however, required meticulous planning; each question had to be carefully crafted if it was to yield the sought-after insight.

Every area of merchandising operations was besieged by this time crunch. Vendor purchase orders needed to be reworked as market forecasts fluctuated. Vendors needed to be kept in the communication loop. Prices needed to be recalculated, gross margins projections adjusted, and profit forecasts modified. All this necessary short-term activity ate up precious hours for Tesija and her team.

Postponing long-term initiatives to devote more time and energy to managing short-term issues sounds like a reasonable solution, but that was not an option. These long-term initiatives were strategically important to Target and could not be shelved, even temporarily.

So how did Tesija deal with the stress of having too much to do? She channeled her adaptive energy to creatively navigate the tension. Recognizing that time was the critical variable, she seized every possible opportunity during problem-solving strategy sessions to make the best use of this scarce resource. In other words, *she made time a focus of her innovation.*

She also carefully reviewed her calendar, made changes that would allow her to use her time more wisely, and encouraged her team to do the same.

With Tesija's promotion came greater accountability and a need to learn and master a seemingly endless number of responsibilities. Over her 25 years with Target, she had been promoted many times, so she was well accustomed to assuming new responsibilities. In the past she had had the luxury of diving deeply into these new areas to make sure she fully understood them while remaining comfortably grounded in more-familiar areas. This time things were different. She had to figure out ways to learn more quickly or risk being overwhelmed.

Tesija accelerated her learning curve by tapping into the expertise of others and by delegating current duties to people she trusted so that she could spend more time familiarizing herself with new areas. Again, Target's culture played a supporting role. One of Target's corporate values, "speed is life," was explained on the Target corporate website like this:

> Target has grown to become America's second-largest retailer through many different successes. Yet, in today's ultra-competitive retail market, each success must fuel the next and speed is essential in the ongoing race to lead the industry. We need to become more efficient, more intelligent and provide guests with the best shopping experience possible both in stores and online.

Target's ambitious corporate philosophy provided Tesija with the cultural support and permission she needed to creatively reconfigure how she deployed her most valuable resource: time.

Tesija's tension map reveals key insights, especially when compared with Joe Dowling's tension map in chapter 4. Unlike Dowling's, Tesija's struggle involved only two tension points—tradition and aspiration—both of which were less intense than Dowling's corresponding tensions. More importantly, it's clear that Tesija's actions reduced tensions, whereas Dowling's actions escalated them.

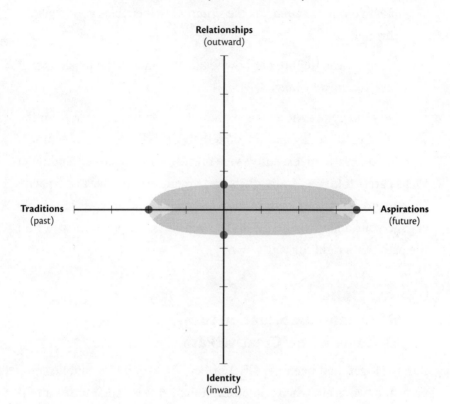

Kathee Tesija's Tension Map

Navigating through Your Tension Map

Recall from part I the two modes of thinking—the automatic mind and the reflective mind. The earlier exercises focused largely on engaging your reflective mind, training it to be more proactive. Here you take the next step: tapping these two different capabilities—automatic and reflective—to work synergistically as you navigate through your tension map.

Two strategies can guide you. Each is explored in depth in the next two sections.

■ *Focus on the situation,* packed full of tension, and think of a creative way to *reimagine the situation* that enables you to get through it.

■ *Focus on you.* Figure out how you contribute to the tensions and *how you might change.*

As you explore these new pathways, try to break loose from the world that exists today and imagine the world that is possible tomorrow. As Kevin Rhein, executive vice president of consumer lending at Wells Fargo, told me, "Individuals and organizations have the capacity far beyond what they believe they are capable of doing." Aim high, engage your adaptive energy, and search for solutions until you find the path that's right for you.

⟨⟩ EXPLORING PRACTICE

Reimagine the Situation to Discover a New Creative Path

Randy Hogan had been the CEO of Pentair, a $3 billion public company, for two years when something unusual was called to his attention. He learned that one of his top lieutenants, a person whom he had personally hired, may have engaged in unethical behavior. Hogan didn't cower or hesitate. He immediately and vigorously investigated; when he determined that the allegations were valid, he promptly fired the individual. That was the easy part.

The aftermath—what Hogan would learn as he investigated the circumstances surrounding the incident—was more problematic. He was shocked to discover that many of the people who worked for this individual were aware of the inappropriate behavior.

When he asked these employees why they hadn't reported their manager's misconduct, the answers were disturbing. Some told Hogan that since he had hired this executive, they assumed that Hogan was aware of and approved of the person's actions. Others said that they were terrified that they would be fired if they blew the whistle.

Hogan told me that this revelation affected him deeply. "It upset me that they didn't know what I valued enough that they would think that," he said. "It hurt, actually. It made me doubt my effectiveness in terms of setting the standards inside the company."

Hogan responded by installing a toll-free hotline so that all employees could anonymously report any future misconduct. But that simple, straightforward solution was only the beginning. Hogan then embarked on a creative path that would have lasting positive impact, both on his own leadership and within the company. In fact, during my interview with him eight years after the fact, it became clear that even *he* had not understood the full ramifications of his actions at the time: "I had a number of all-employee meetings. I got up in front of folks and I apologized. I told them, 'Half of you wanted to tell me what was going on but couldn't, and the other half didn't believe I would care. I want you all to look me in the eye and know that I would rather lose right than win wrong. But what we are all about is 'winning right.'"

That heartfelt speech was a breakthrough moment. Hogan's phrase of "winning right" would become a company mantra, realigning corporate values and laying the groundwork for long-term success. "At the time I did not realize that it was an opportunity for solidifying what was an unspoken sense into a statement of purpose. That statement is something that we now reinforce all the time."

An unexpected consequence of this struggle episode was that it helped Hogan articulate his own values as a leader. He told me that he had initially been attracted to Pentair because of its strong system of values. He especially appreciated that his predecessor had wanted to build a "high-performance company with a heart." "I came aboard really liking that concept," he said, "but I had never really made the heart part my own. It was already here, part of the culture. I had never been able to make it my own until I had the opportunity to articulate what it meant to me."

Suddenly, with "winning right," Hogan was able to viscerally internalize those values. Doing so enabled him to kick his leadership into high gear and tackle some difficult and thorny problems. One such problem was Pentair's long tradition of decentralization:

> One of the struggles was that we were basically a holding company, decentralized. And decentralization was one of the cultural totems that each of the individual businesses held dear. Of all the Pentair values, their independence was the most important to them. But to me it was an irrelevant value because it had nothing to do with high performance or with treating people with dignity and respect. And it didn't allow us to go global. It was something that I had to dismantle essentially.

Even though Hogan had recognized this problem early on in his tenure as CEO, the organization had resisted his early efforts to confront these tensions of tradition. "Everything I did was considered an attack on decentralization," he said.

The "winning right" mantra gave permission for Hogan to initiate a new conversation around this sensitive topic. "Decentralization didn't have anything to do with winning right," he noted. Thus this new yardstick for success—winning right—built the foundation for a new corporate culture, encapsulating the dream that attracted him to the company: a high-performance company with a heart.

Hogan's experience illustrates how a number of concepts in this book can be practically applied. His story begins with the stumble/recover/learn script. As Hogan began to doubt his effectiveness in setting internal company standards, his reflective mind told him to pay attention; something was not quite right.

As the script unfolded, Hogan's adaptive energy kicked in. Summoned by the reflective mind's call to action, Hogan reimagined the situation and conceived a fresh new approach: a three-tiered hierarchy of values. At the lowest level was *winning wrong,* the worst of all outcomes, one that Hogan would do anything to avoid. More preferred was *losing right.* Hogan didn't want to lose, but he preferred losing the right way to winning the wrong way. At the top of the hierarchy was *winning right.* This two-word motto, which epitomized the ultimate criteria for success, would come to embody the company's highest aspirations.

With the emergence of winning right, Hogan moved on from the stumble/recover/learn script as the ripples of his creative brainstorm extended beyond what he had imagined possible. As he began following the transcending-constraint script, he saw an opportunity to legitimately dismantle the culture of decentralization, a previous constraint on corporate performance.

Hogan's intuitive leap exemplifies the mind-set of an experienced leader. After embracing struggle and navigating tensions, he discovered a creative solution that would surprise even him with its far-reaching effects.

Reflective Exercise: Reimagine Your Situation

Now it is your turn. Try to envision a pathway through whatever challenges you're facing. To get started, consider the following questions:

- *Have you suffered a setback like Hogan did?* If so, it's natural to experience some negative emotions. Take a little time to acknowledge them. Now, using the ABC exercise from chapter 3, examine the underlying beliefs that led to the emotions. These could be beliefs about what caused the setback to happen and what it might mean for your future. Now think of some more adaptive beliefs that you can substitute.

- *Do you feel somewhat drained of energy or disengaged?* If so, it's possible that your struggle is affecting you at a deeper level. Here's a two-pronged approach that might help: First, do something; take some small step forward, even if it seems inconsequential. Second, make sure you read the next three chapters. It's possible that some element of your job is out of alignment with your core purpose in life. The pages that follow may shed some light on this for you.

■ *Do you need new skills to mount the challenge?* If this is the case, remind yourself of the growth mind-set explained in chapter 3. You *can* "wake up smarter tomorrow" if you proactively work at it. There are numerous ways to build your skills. You can take courses, attend seminars, and read books, like Rita Marshall did—or you can do what Kate Herzog did and seek out successful external models or find people to whom to delegate certain tasks.

■ *Do you feel that the pressures of the short term are keeping you from important long-term tasks?* Author Stephen Covey popularized a time management matrix that consisted of four quadrants: *important urgent, important not urgent, not important urgent,* and *not important not urgent.* He recommended clearing all the not important stuff off your plate so that you have more time to deal with the important issues, urgent or not. In essence this is what Kathee Tesija did by clarifying what was truly important and then making clear choices about how she and her team could best use their time. Tesija's experience drives home the point that deciding what *not* to do can be as valuable as deciding what to do.

■ *Do the obstacles ahead make you question whether your goals are really attainable?* In any difficult situation, there are bound to be times where you don't see a clear path to your goal—or the path you do see is obscured by roadblocks and minefields. Perhaps different people have different visions for the future, with those disagreements diverting energy away from charging forward. It may be that organizational incentives are not aligned with what the organization has asked you to do. Sometimes, as in the case of Sandy Jones, the stretch goals set by senior management are simply unattainable.

Whatever is going on, the key is aligning your adaptive energy to break out of old habits and expand the menu of alternatives you consider. You might find it helpful to act on one of the two grounding practices discussed in chapter 5: Find people to talk to—a coach or mentor, your boss, your peers, your team, your family, or your circle of friends. Just talking about the problem may help you see new solutions you had not previously envisioned. Also, you can turn your mind inward. Find a meditation that will allow you to connect with your inner self and nurture your creativity. Or find a peaceful place and just be there in full awareness. Sometimes, when you step away from a problem instead of focusing on it, a fresh alternative suddenly presents itself. Whether you try one of these approaches or a combination of both, a new creative idea may emerge that will help you take the next step on your journey.

⊕ EXPLORING PRACTICE

Reinvent Yourself

Several times the US Army tried to entice Captain Joe Kelly to transfer from the field artillery branch to the armor (tank) branch. Captain Kelly refused every offer. He was an artillery guy. His father was an artillery guy. So was his brother. Everyone knows that you don't just change colors (army jargon for branches) that easily. Finally, the army made him an irresistible offer and Captain Kelly accepted, beginning an odyssey of growth and awakening that set the stage for a series of accelerated promotions that culminated with his ascendance to general.

Kelly, who grew up in a blue-collar family, studied accounting in college, and through the Reserve Officer Training Corps was commissioned as a second lieutenant of field artillery soon after graduation. He quickly distinguished himself as an artillery officer, finishing first in his officer basic course class among more than 120 lieutenants and receiving multiple awards. He advanced steadily in the artillery career field and was promoted to captain in his late twenties.

That's when the opportunity came for him to change specialties and command a 100-soldier tank company as a captain in the armor branch. Kelly explained to me the differences between these two branches and the challenges he faced in making the switch:

> Field artillery is synonymous with cannons and combat support. Picture a unit with a bunch of cannons behind the front lines shooting cannonballs against the enemy in support of the infantry guys—the combat forces up front. It tends to be a very scientific branch, driven by drill and standard operating procedure. To a field artillery officer, it does not matter whether it is day or night, arctic or desert, rain or snow. You do the same things all the time. You go to wherever on the earth you are supposed to be, get yourself oriented, and then start providing fire support.
>
> The armor guys are what we in the military call a "maneuver branch." They are the soldiers whose job it is to go and find the enemy and accomplish whatever it is they need to. They are the frontline troops. Armor is much more fluid than artillery because you are reacting not only to yourself and the terrain but also to what the enemy is doing.
>
> Normally the military does a fabulous job of preparing you for the next assignment down the road in your career, but I had been trained and conditioned to be the commander of an artillery unit. And suddenly I was commanding a tank unit. So I was trying to do the job of company commander without the benefit of having been a lieutenant, platoon leader, and unit executive officer. I just jumped right in without really knowing what we did and how to do it.

Kelly admits that it was "kind of scary" to make the change. His job had always been scientific and structured. Now he was in a chaotic, uncontrolled, and unstructured world.

The move was difficult from another perspective as well. Kelly had always considered himself a perfectionist, somebody who through preparation and perspiration would always win the day. He built his whole leadership identity around that image:

> I wanted to have this bulletproof persona. I wanted to be an all-knowing, follow-me, perfect kind of leader who knew exactly what he was doing. I had a philosophy about leadership that said that competence—technical confidence in the task at hand—was one of the most, if not the most, important leadership traits that would inspire people to follow you. I was once expounding on this to young officers. I said, "Who would want to follow somebody who doesn't know what they're doing?" And then I became somebody who didn't know what the hell he was doing.

There was one more factor that made Kelly's transition difficult: he was transplanted into a completely new and different social system. "I went from a cohort of officers that I had grown up with to plugging in socially to another cohort of guys who are looking at me like, 'Who is this cat? Who does he know, and why did he get that job?' I had to establish a whole bunch of new relationships from zero. In a tribe where most of the relationships had been formed when they were lieutenants, I was the new kid in school."

Kelly described the change as "humbling." He knew that no matter how hard he tried, he would never be better technically than those who had come up through the ranks in the armor branch. He had to learn everything from scratch, including rethinking the fundamental role of leadership itself.

From the start, Kelly approached his new leadership assignment differently than he had in the past. As soon as the opportunity presented itself, he got up in front of his unit and said:

I'm not going to bullshit you. This is all new to me. I have a lot to
learn. You know more about what we do than I do, so I need to
learn from you. I need to learn the nuts and bolts of what we do.
And I need your help to do it. Having said that, fellas, don't be
confused about who is in charge. Don't be confused about who
is responsible for what we do or fail to do. I am just telling you,
I have a lot to learn and I need your help.

Kelly made a special point of training with his unit and always
being right in the middle of everything, in full view of his troops. He
admitted that it was a risky move because if he failed, he'd be failing in
front of his entire unit. But there was another reason he made himself
so visible. "By diving into the middle of something, I was able to pick
it up," he explained. "Once you start doing, you start understanding."
That approach also allowed him to form more-personal relationships
with his troops as he worked side by side with them.

Integrity and Caring

Kelly's most dramatic change, the one that would propel his career
forward, was rooted in the way he thought about leadership. He liter-
ally reinvented himself as a leader, washing away old, outdated models
and adopting new ideas about what makes a good leader. In place of
technical competence, Kelly began to value integrity and caring as the
most important leadership traits. He told me: "They will not follow
you if they do not believe that you are an honest, trustworthy person
of integrity who is going to take care of them and do the right things."

Kelly reinvented one additional aspect of his leadership model.
He purged, as best he could, his old self-concept as a perfectionist, replacing it with a priority on valuing relationships and people:
"I went from valuing the immediate result to valuing the people I was
with. I learned the power of letting go a little bit, of not needing to be
in control, of relying on other people and trusting someone else to do
something or to help me. Instead of being shy and inwardly focused,

I transitioned to *I really like people*. And that's what was important in the end."

When I interviewed Kelly, he had achieved the rank of general. His rapid rise through the ranks, in his estimation, stemmed largely from his growth and development in this pivotal assignment. He described it as an "awakening" of sorts, a shift of personality from being a "relatively shy, quiet, careful person to one who is much more outgoing, more willing to step out, less concerned about being prepared, and more interested in developing the situation." Kelly drew the parallel of his personality shift to the personality differences of the branches themselves. His assignment in armor had awakened a new aspect of his personality that had lain dormant during his time in the artillery branch.

Kelly's metamorphosis can be more fully appreciated by focusing on three aspects of his story. First, Kelly seemed to intuitively anticipate the type of shift required by his new career field of armor. He paid attention to the fact that he was in a radically different specialty with radically different criteria for success. Recognizing that the strategies he had used in the past would not work in this new environment, he left himself open to change.

A second element of interest was the nature of Kelly's shift, occurring at levels fundamental to his identity, leadership philosophy, and personality. Consciously or not, Kelly decided to adapt to his environment rather than try to change it. His energies were thus focused inward, discerning how he could best change himself in response to the change of external realities.

A third element was the nature of Kelly's emotions. Yes, his new situation was a little scary. In retrospect, however, he described himself as "humbled," which he carefully distinguished from feeling "humiliated." In a situation like Kelly's, it would be easy to let the ego take over, ceding control to negative emotions and fanning the flames of self-doubt. To his credit, Kelly kept his negative emotions in check, focusing all of his energy on creating adaptive strategies.

These three attributes make Kelly's story a good case study of the proactive-reinvention script. He navigated through this struggle episode by transforming tensions into adaptive energy, fundamentally changing himself as a leader.

Reflective Exercise: Reinventing Yourself to Adapt to Your Current Situation

Once again it's time for you to think about your own situation. In your notebook, write down your answers to these questions:

- Are my old models and styles of leadership working for me right now?

- What do I need to change about myself to better adapt to my current situation?

As a starting place, refer back to the exercise in chapter 3 where you listed behaviors that are adaptive and those that interfere with your effective functioning. Now look one level deeper to probe the underlying models, assumptions, and philosophies that frame your leadership. As illustrated several times so far, leadership growth often means shedding outdated approaches in exchange for newer, more adaptive ones. As Microsoft grew through the 1980s, Bill Gates's long-held leadership model—that technical leaders should always report to someone more technically qualified—began to lose validity. Thus he inverted the hierarchy by accepting the need for a cadre of business unit general managers, setting the stage for a new phase of company growth.

In chapter 4 Joe Dowling took his leadership to the next level at the Guthrie Theater by becoming more inclusive in his leadership style—shifting his worldview from "I" to "we." In this chapter Joe Kelly jettisoned a leadership model that prized technical know-how toward a new understanding favoring integrity, genuine caring, and relationships. Through Kelly's metamorphosis he not only adapted to his current situation but also set the stage for his rapid rise to general.

All of these remarkable transformations were sparked by some underlying tension that acted as a catalyst for change. Take a look at the tension map you drew in chapter 4. What is it telling you? What old models and assumptions do you need to let go of to make space for new, more adaptive ones? What do you need to change about *yourself* to better adapt to the circumstances in which you find yourself?

Of course, if your current struggle is particularly intense, you may be quietly asking yourself, *Do I really want to adapt to my current situation? Wouldn't it be better to find a different situation?* If this feeling is a strong one, spend some time reflecting on it, perhaps by writing about your feelings in your notebook. Chapter 9 delves deeper into this question, but first there is much ground to cover. In the meantime you might consider some mini-experiments to collect more data and come to a deeper and more comprehensive understanding of your current circumstances. For example, try to identify a behavior you're engaging in that may be creating unnecessary tension in your workplace, then consciously work to put a stop to it. You may be surprised to see how a situation cools down when you stop stoking the fire.

7

Illuminate Blind Spots

*Human madness is oftentimes a cunning and most
feline thing. When you think it fled, it may have but
become transfigured into some still subtler form.*

— Herman Melville, *Moby-Dick*

YEARS AGO, NOT LONG AFTER RECEIVING MY DRIVER'S LICENSE, I
merged onto a freeway. Needing to move into the left lane, I flipped
on my signal and glanced in the side-view mirror. I didn't see any cars,
so I started changing lanes. Suddenly, I was jolted by an angry horn.
Whipping my head to my left, I saw a red-faced driver pounding his
horn and yelling at me through closed windows. I had almost cut right
in front of him.

He had been invisible to me because he was perfectly positioned
in my blind spot, the precise area that my car mirrors couldn't pick up.
I had forgotten a critical lesson from driver's education class: *Always
physically turn your head to look in your blind spot before you change
lanes.* Fortunately, the other driver's quick reflexes averted an accident,
but the incident shook me up so much that I vowed never again to be
so lax behind the wheel.

Leadership blind spots are no different. Unless you proactively
look for your blind spot, you may drift into the wrong lane and col-
lide with unpleasant circumstances. Joe Dowling's story in chapter 4
described how his blind spot—a consequence of his being too confrontational—led to missed opportunities when he was the Abbey
Theatre's artistic director. Fortunately, a colleague's comment later in
his career shocked him into awareness of this blind spot. With greater

wisdom and humility, Dowling transformed himself as a leader and took his work to a higher level.

Blind spots are the product of an overactive automatic mind and an underactive reflective mind. In my freeway example, my automatic mind had not been sufficiently conditioned to appreciate the importance of physically checking out my blind spot before changing lanes. My reflective mind stayed out of the way and let whatever was going to happen, happen. Once I heard the blast of the horn, my reflective mind reasserted itself and demanded that I relearn and honor the correct protocol for changing lanes. I'm sure that wasn't the first time I failed to turn my head before changing lanes, but I can assure you it was the last time. My automatic mind now reminds me of this lifesaving requirement every time I turn on my blinker, leaving my reflective mind free to focus on other things.

For the purposes of this book, I'm defining a *blind spot* as anything that can hinder or undermine your performance that you are either unaware of or have chosen to overlook. My research has identified five different types of blind spots: experience, personality, values, strategic, and conflict.

Experience Blind Spots: Success Is a Lousy Teacher

In *The Road Ahead,* Bill Gates wrote, "Success is a lousy teacher. It seduces smart people into thinking they can't lose." One reason for this is the experience blind spot.

Nothing boosts our confidence like success. Rarely do we delve into a nuanced reflective analysis of what led to the successful outcome, including the role of luck. Instead the strategies and the tactics we used along with the confidence we gained become generically encoded into the automatic mind. When we encounter a new situation, we may spontaneously draw on this menu without questioning whether these strategies are appropriate for the new circumstances.

The irony is that a long history of accolades and achievements could potentially produce troublesome blind spots.

Roger MacMillan's story exemplifies the danger in assuming that past results guarantee future success. MacMillan, who began his career as a consultant, was recruited into a staff job for a large chain of fast-food restaurants. The new job was similar to his consulting role in many respects, and he enjoyed significant success. Soon he was promoted into a line management position, overseeing the operations of a large number of restaurants. That's when things started to go haywire.

Unlike MacMillan, all of those who reported directly to him were restaurant operations people who had come up through the ranks. MacMillan's boss was a seasoned operations executive as well. MacMillan was selected for his new role because the company wanted to tap his exceptional process design skills, which MacMillan had learned as a consultant. Theoretically, it was a reasonable expectation.

MacMillan's boss and direct reports soon learned that MacMillan's approach and philosophy were very different from theirs. An operations person typically has a short-term outlook. When an operational problem is brought to light, the operating folks want to fix it quickly and be done with it. MacMillan's training and experience, however, taught him the value of analyzing every conceivable aspect of a problem to ensure that a short-term solution would be the right choice for the long term as well. Whenever MacMillan's direct reports wanted to dive in and change something, MacMillan would hold them back, telling them to wait until the situation was properly analyzed. Problems that previously could be solved within hours now took weeks to resolve. MacMillan's boss encountered the same resistance. When he asked for a quick change in procedure, MacMillan would drag out the process for what seemed like an eternity to this fast-moving organization.

Meanwhile, MacMillan did not pick up on any of the multitudes of subtle cues that were directed his way. He thought everything was working as it should be, and he dismissed negative feedback as evidence that his critics just didn't know what they were talking about. After all, he had been brought into the role specifically for his great process skills. In his mind he was rewarding the company's trust in him by providing them with the professional services they were looking for.

MacMillan's direct reports had a different view. They started going around him and dealing directly with his boss, who had actually been their boss until MacMillan had been inserted into the mix. The direct reports found a sympathetic ear in their former boss, who was as fed up with MacMillan's paralysis by analysis as they were.

It didn't take long for the frustration of MacMillan's colleagues to reach critical mass. Instead of taking the time to understand the discontent that was swirling around him, MacMillan autocratically asserted his authority over his direct reports, which made a bad situation worse. As tensions reached the breaking point, MacMillan was moved out of his role and placed in a position with significantly less authority. Feeling the classic symptoms of burnout, he ended up leaving the company.

MacMillan's story is a classic case study of the experience blind spot. His past experience as a consultant and process expert blinded him to the requirements and the expectations of the operations role. He wasn't intuitive enough to sense the different nature of his new environment. He wasn't agile enough to realize that what worked in the past would not work in his new assignment. He wasn't resourceful enough to find a way to bring his process expertise to his operations role and make his direct reports, as well as his former boss, his partners in the endeavor. He wasn't empathetic enough to acknowledge the growing relationship tensions and to ask for his colleagues' help, which might have made all the difference. Although he was receiving feedback and constructive criticism, MacMillan didn't pay enough attention to anyone's complaints or concerns until it was too late.

He was narrowly focused, overconfident in his ability to handle things, and unwilling to acknowledge that he had anything to learn.

MacMillan's reflective mind failed him on three counts. First, it submissively allowed his automatic mind to think it had all the answers. Second, it did not even consider that there might be a conflict between operational philosophies. Third, it did not pay adequate attention to a plethora of early warning signs. Unlike Captain Joe Kelly in chapter 6, who understood that openly admitting he had much to learn and training side by side with his unit would earn their respect, MacMillan played the authoritarian card. Kelly intuitively understood that to lead he needed to learn and adapt in his new environment.

Such thoughts apparently never crossed MacMillan's mind. Because the proactive-reinvention script wasn't even on his radar, MacMillan wasn't able to adapt to his new situation. Nor did he follow the stumble/recover/learn script, which would have alerted him to the problem and guided him to take corrective action. Instead he tuned out, held out, and burned out.

The experience blind spot is most likely to come into play when leaders move to a new role or a new company. They arrive so eager to show off what they know that they don't pay close enough attention to their new circumstances. The experience blind spot can also be problematic when leaders have become entrenched in a job and something significant changes in the environment. The risk in such a scenario is that they continue on autopilot without noticing the need for radical change. Their automatic mind continues to tell them that all is well, and their reflective mind is too lazy to blow the whistle.

Personality Blind Spots:
The Ghost behind the Strength

Personality blind spots can manifest in similar ways. Just as past experience can produce tunnel vision in leaders who are not self-aware enough to notice it, the structure of your personality—your predisposition to think and act in certain ways—can lead you to erroneously process information and miss subtle cues unless you are self-aware enough to monitor your thoughts and make appropriate course corrections.

Every personality type has its own set of assets and a corresponding blind spot. For example, affable people may be more friendly and engaging but may be overly loyal and avoid necessary conflict. People who are deliberate and methodical may be more precise in their work but may be slow to take action.

Marc Belton, the General Mills executive who sought out an executive coach, told me that he considers personality blind spots the "ghost behind the strength" because these blind spots are typically associated with personality traits that would normally be considered strengths. Belton, for example, scores particularly high on a scale that measures imagination and creativity, personality assets that are valuable at General Mills because of the company's focus on innovation. He is also aware of the "ghost" side of his personality—the tendency to favor right-brain thinking (intuition) over left-brain thinking (logic)— especially now that he has moved into higher levels of responsibility.

Belton has trained himself to recognize the early warning signs of potential conflicts related to these thought-process differences. When colleagues have difficulty seeing the connections that he makes intuitively, he focuses on creating clear, concise, logical arguments that help people "connect the dots." Similarly, when a proposal that Belton has advocated for isn't adopted, he reminds himself to go back and rethink his assumptions while factoring in the views of others. Sometimes when he finds himself in "a strange place when I'm not quite sure what's going on," he asks himself, *Am I playing to the ghost side of my strength?* Checking in with himself like this reminds him of the need for whole-brain thinking. Ultimately, this increased self-awareness leads to higher-quality interactions and decisions.

Dick Schulze, founder and former CEO of Best Buy, told me that he became aware of his blind spot early in his career, when a personality test showed that he had a "controlling personality." Despite the negative-sounding name, this type of personality is imbued with many strengths, including a penchant for being passionate, relentless, bold, and outspoken. Still, its ghost side carries with it certain risks, including the tendency to be so overconfident in one's own analysis and plans that one does not seek input and advice from others.

To Schulze, recognizing this blind spot was a turning point in his life and career. "That's when the bell went off, and I said, 'You know, I just better come off my high horse and understand that I don't have all the answers,'" he told me. "I better start listening to people around me and try to understand their points of view. And I dedicated myself to being the best listener ever." During our interview Schulze emphasized his inclusive approach to leadership, which was a direct result of the work he put into overcoming this blind spot.

Nine months after I initially interviewed Schulze, something happened that would reveal just how powerful blind spots can be. Someone brought to Schulze a report that Best Buy's then-CEO, Brian Dunn, may have engaged in an inappropriate relationship with a female employee. Schulze confronted Dunn with the report, which Dunn emphatically denied. Schulze told Dunn that the observations made in the report were clearly in violation of company policy and, if they continued, would go to a higher level of review. Schulze then dropped the matter without telling anyone else.

Subsequently, the matter came to light through other channels, and the board launched a formal investigation. Although no laws were broken, the investigation concluded that Dunn's relationship with the employee had violated company policy and that Schulze should have promptly informed the Audit Committee or other officials. The incident forced Schulze to resign as chair.

I spoke with Schulze again about six weeks after he resigned. He strongly defended his actions, saying that a majority of Executive Board chairs would have done the same thing. But then I asked him what he would do differently if he had it to do over again. He candidly told me that he would have brought Best Buy's chief counsel into the loop immediately after confronting Dunn, seeking his advice on whether any other action was appropriate. I asked him why he didn't take that action at the time, and he said that it simply did not occur to him.

Schulze's story offers a deeper understanding of blind spots on multiple levels. Blind spots not only restrict the range of options considered but also create a bias toward actions that may be suboptimal, even for a leader as accomplished as Schulze, who had built a $50 billion company. Blind spots are also persistent. Even though Schulze had long been vigilant about keeping his blind spot in check, on this occasion it simply snuck past his defenses.

It is of course unknowable what would have happened had Schulze consulted with Best Buy's chief counsel after confronting Dunn, but the events that did play out would set Schulze and Best Buy on a radically different trajectory; that story continues in chapter 9.

Values Blind Spots

"It was the loneliest night of my life," Frank Russomanno recalled. He was alone in a hotel room on a business trip and had just received a call from an Imation board member telling him that he had not been selected to be Imation's next CEO. Instead they wanted him to remain on as the chief operating officer, the number two position in the company.

"That was the longest night of my life because I wasn't at home," he told me. "I didn't have my wife. I spent it in this dark hotel room in Boston. The next day I got up and did my presentation to all these analysts. I didn't act any differently around the guy I was traveling with because no one could know. I could not wait to get home that Friday. All the venting started on Friday night after the plane landed in Minneapolis."

Russomanno had spent most of his career at 3M. When Imation spun off from 3M, he went over to Imation and had worked his way up to COO. By his own account, he was content at Imation; he had a great relationship with the CEO, Bill Monahan, and felt valued and respected.

When Monahan announced his retirement, Russomanno interviewed for the job. Then came the phone call at the Boston hotel, which was followed by three weeks of anguish and resentment: "When Bill said he was leaving, I said there's no reason why I can't do his job. And then they brought in someone who had no experience in the industry—none—and had no feel for the transition the company was going through. I was ready to resign and cast my lot somewhere else."

Because he was a high-ranking official at Imation, Russomanno had to be careful not to display any angst about being passed over. He did his best to come across as a positive team player. His wife was his primary support. After he spent three weeks moping around and feeling sorry for himself at home, his wife asked him two simple questions: First she asked, "If Bill Monahan was still CEO, would you stay with the company?" Russomanno had to concede that he would stay.

And then his wife asked the pivotal question: "How can you leave when you talk so much about caring about the company, its direction, and most of all the people who work in the company? Because at the end of the day, the company is people."

Her poignant question and insight helped Russomanno gain clarity about the right course of action. He decided to stay and work with the new CEO as his number two. Russomanno said, "In the end the values were more important than my ego and desire to be CEO."

When I asked Russomanno what was going on in his mind during those three weeks, he told me:

I think that I was out of balance. Ego was running me. I was too "me" oriented. When I didn't get the job, I thought I was short-changed. I didn't think they saw all the good things I'd done for the company.

Those thoughts were atypical of me because they were all about myself. I'm not like that, so it was very uncomfortable for me. I don't like a lot of attention directed toward me. I like to succeed and win and do all those things, but at that time I was pretty self-consumed and upset that the board didn't get it right.

So the balance was off. And if you go out of balance as a leader, you can be very flawed. That's why my wife's second question was so important. I could not walk around all these years saying that I care about this company and I care about the people and then, just because I didn't get a job, walk away. Now other people could've done that. But that wasn't me. And that was a real struggle for me, I have to tell you that.

Russomanno's wife called his attention to a critical inconsistency in his identity as a leader. His craving to become CEO was instigated by his ego when his boss resigned. When he didn't get the job, his ego goaded him into a prolonged state of righteous indignation. Yet all of that was inconsistent with his core values, which had become the bedrock of his leadership identity. During those agonizing three weeks, Russomanno was so off balance that he was blind to this incongruity. He didn't realize that his attitude and emotions were out of sync with his values until his wife brought it to his attention.

Once Russomanno's blind spot became illuminated, he could shift his thinking, regain his balance, and reimagine the situation in a way that gave voice to his core values. He settled in again as COO and developed a great working relationship with the new CEO, Bruce Henderson.

Through working with Henderson, Russomanno learned additional skills that helped him become a more well-rounded executive.

Russomanno's area of expertise was operations, whereas Henderson had extensive experience in strategic thinking and planning.

Russomanno told me: "I was happy. I was comfortable. I saw Bruce as a good guy. I liked him personally. I can remember thinking: *This is where I'm going to retire. I'm making good money. I'm the number two guy in the company. I'm trusted. I'm on public boards. Life ain't bad.*"

And that's when life threw another curveball. Several years into his tenure as CEO, Henderson learned he had a malignant brain tumor; it was a glioblastoma, a very serious form of cancer. The board asked Russomanno to lead the company as acting CEO during Henderson's absence and then officially named Russomanno CEO several months later. Bruce Henderson died soon thereafter. Russomanno remained CEO until he retired in 2010.

Values blind spots occur when a leader's attitude and actions are not aligned with core values. Russomanno was fortunate that his wife helped bring his blind spot to his conscious awareness so that he could directly confront and then correct the misalignment.

Unfortunately, not all values blind spots become illuminated in time, and some can have far-reaching consequences. Joe Paterno, the legendary Pennsylvania State University football coach, exhibited a tragic lapse of judgment when he failed to take sufficient action after discovering that Jerry Sandusky, his former assistant coach, may have engaged in improper relationships with children.

Until this sordid affair came to light, Paterno had been considered a model leader and an icon of integrity and rectitude. For decades he was known and applauded for actively preaching and practicing high moral standards, insisting on rigid conformance to accepted rules, encouraging athletes to excel academically as well as athletically, and generously donating his money to charity. In January 2012 Paterno died at 85 under a cloud of controversy. Less than six months later, revelations in former FBI Director Louis Freeh's report on the

Penn State scandal about what Paterno knew and when he knew it left Paterno's reputation in ashes.

Remember, a blind spot doesn't necessarily mean that you are unaware of a problem; blinds spots can occur even if you have some level of awareness but fail to take appropriate action. According to the Freeh report, Paterno chose to cover up the reported abuse to keep the school's reputation intact. Inevitably, the approach backfired, damaging the reputation not only of Penn State but also of Paterno and other senior school officials. Lost in the media firestorm over the scandal is Paterno's otherwise exceptional record of achievement and positive influence on generations of young men. By the time Paterno died, his good works had been overshadowed by this stunning breach of his stated values, saddening the hearts of family, friends, and admirers.

The Penn State ordeal is notable because in addition to Paterno's individual blind spot, there are also institutional implications. Powerful incentives were at work that influenced Paterno, other Penn State administrators, and, arguably, the institution of college football itself. Implicit incentives to maintain the status quo within an institution or organization can be one of the indicators of a strategic blind spot.

Strategic Blind Spots

The three blind spots discussed so far—experience, personality, and values—focused largely on individual failings. Strategic blind spots cast a wider net because their influence is felt on a larger level, affecting a group, a company, or an institution. They are products of a collective worldview that becomes self-reinforcing around a set of practices, assumptions, or beliefs yet are potentially maladaptive for the long-term health of the organization. There are often incentives, either explicit or implicit, that reward conformance to the norm and punish critical or questioning voices. These incentives, which often are tied to short-term objectives, can detract attention from critical long-term implications, hindering open, honest dialogue and cogent analysis.

The Penn State football scandal is an instructive example of a strategic blind spot. It would have taken considerable courage to blow the whistle on Jerry Sandusky because doing so could have jeopardized the multimillion-dollar business that is Penn State football. So instead of taking bold action, the many individuals with knowledge of Sandusky's actions sat passively by and allegedly allowed the abuse to continue. It appears that many automatic minds were working in concert, unconsciously conspiring to hobble their corresponding reflective minds from doing what was right.

Strategic blind spots can occur in virtually any area of an organization and are not necessarily restricted to values, as in the Penn State example. Any initiative, practice, or custom is a potential focus point. My own experience at Microsoft in the mideighties affirms that not all strategic blind spot stories end badly.

As I transitioned into my job as general manager of the development tools business for Microsoft in 1985, the BASIC team was working on what was, at the time, called Windows BASIC. Bill Gates and Steve Ballmer had crafted this strategy as part of a companywide initiative in support of the Windows 1.0 launch later that year, a plan that envisioned the graphical user interface to be the future of computing and of Microsoft. It seemed clear to everybody that this was the right path; after all, Microsoft had gone all in on the GUI, and the prevailing wisdom was that anything that could be done to make this strategy successful absolutely needed to be done.

In my new role, I conducted a thorough review of all projects. By the time I finished, I had concluded that things weren't quite adding up. My team's main mission was to defend against an attack by Borland International, which still operated in the non-GUI, character-based world. Instead of exploiting the newest graphical interface technology, Borland's strategy focused on being superfast, which is why its customers loved it. Programs running in the GUI world on the IBM PC, circa 1985, were very slow. Back then even the fastest computers still used the 286 chip, a virtual tortoise by today's standards. Market dynamics dictated that if Microsoft were to release a Windows-based BASIC product at that time, it would have been crushed by Borland in the marketplace; it would simply be too slow.

The mismatch was clear to me as was the course of action we needed to take. We had to stop work on Windows BASIC and start work on a faster non-GUI product that could compete with Borland—we simply didn't have the resources to do both. But could I get Bill Gates and Steve Ballmer to agree to jettison BASIC from the Windows mother ship?

Bill was first to buy in, and I think he finally convinced Steve, who remained wary for a few more weeks. We temporarily shelved Windows BASIC and immediately launched a new initiative. Within two years we had dealt Borland a deathblow. When the time was right, the BASIC team picked back up on their GUI efforts, ultimately producing Visual BASIC, a product that remains on the market today.

Even though there had been a strategic blind spot, Bill and Steve gave me the charter to see things from a different perspective, and to their credit they listened to me when I brought my concerns to their attention. My questions made us all pause to reflect and reexamine, bringing explicit dialogue and debate to strategy issues that had previously been hidden and unchallenged. In this case we were fortunate that our revised strategy was successful. A decade later, however, I would have another bout with the strategic blind spot where things didn't work out so well.

In 1996 I became CEO of Net Perceptions, a Minneapolis company I also co-founded. We commercialized a technology called collaborative filtering, which originated at the University of Minnesota. This technology was used to recommend things to online users that they might like based on the preferences of other people with similar profiles.

Back then the promise of one-to-one relationships with customers via the Internet was a revolutionary concept, so collaborative filtering, the vehicle for personalization, became quite hot. One of our early customers was Amazon. I traveled to Seattle to personally sell Amazon founder Jeff Bezos, and we developed a good working relationship.

One day Jeff called me with an offer that he was excited about. He asked us to work with Amazon exclusively in the book area for 18 months. If we agreed not to sell to any other book merchants, he would pay us a small amount of cash. He also offered to personally serve as a reference to a certain number of our nonbook-related prospects.

At our next Net Perceptions board meeting, I brought Jeff's offer up as an agenda item. One executive on my management team spoke forcefully against Jeff's proposal. He said we didn't need Jeff Bezos to sell our products, and he pointed to several potential deals in the pipeline with Barnes & Noble, Borders, and Ingram that were worth a considerable amount of money. A venture capital board member voiced quick agreement, asking, "Does anybody think this is anything but a no-brainer?" Everyone in the room fell silent, including me.

When I look back on this decision, I realize it was anything but a no-brainer; it was a strategic blind spot. Absent from the all-too-brief debate that day were two factors that, in the final analysis, would loom larger than the financial issues that had leapt to the forefront. One was the quality of the relationship with Amazon. Amazon was looking for a business partner, not a vendor. It was looking to establish a competitive advantage in the book market and saw our product as a vehicle to accomplish this. What's more, because our product was at an early stage of development, the Amazon technical staff felt that they would need to make a significant contribution to help advance our product's capabilities to meet their needs.

The second factor that was not given adequate attention was that we too needed Amazon as a business partner. Amazon was offering itself as a willing test lab that would take early product releases, test them at scale, and give us feedback. In the drive to grow revenues, we failed to recognize the importance of acquiring a fully vested customer partner of Amazon's stature to help us develop our product and delivery capabilities.

The blind spot stemmed from the inherent nature of our industry. As a venture-backed Internet startup in the mid-1990s, the company had a top priority to grow revenues and go public as quickly as possible. Alan Greenspan, then chair of the Federal Reserve Board, tacitly endorsed this approach when he described access to the public markets as a "Darwinian" process. Once we went public, we would have access to more capital, which would allow us to grow faster.

The incentive structure of the venture capital industry was also a factor. The quicker a company went public, the faster the venture capitalists who invested in the company could realize a profit on their investment. We had excellent and farsighted venture capital board members. Still, those hard-to-argue-with incentives combined with the reality of "Darwinian" capital markets permeated through all startups of our vintage.

When I called Jeff Bezos to tell him of our decision, he sounded disappointed. Ultimately, Amazon's leaders decided that this technology was so critical to their strategy that they could not risk its becoming a commodity, so they ramped up an internal effort to build their own collaborative filtering capability; consequently, our relationship with Amazon languished.

Ironically, while we did ultimately realize some revenue from those other booksellers, it was nothing near what we had imagined on the day we made the Amazon decision. Still, on balance, we exceeded our financial goals, at least in the short term, and had a successful initial public offering and secondary offering. But when the Internet bust hit, we had not yet built up the proven customer value proposition that might have sustained us over the long term, and the company was sold.

With the benefit of hindsight, I can see that the decision was much more complicated than had been considered at the time. Analysis had zeroed in on the immediate financial considerations without weighing other factors. Had I presented a more balanced picture to the board, other alternatives might have surfaced. After hearing Jeff's disappointment on the phone, I might have personally flown to Seattle to meet with him face to face; perhaps I would have gained a keener insight into his hopes for the relationship, and things would have turned out differently.

Conflict Blind Spots

This last blind spot takes center stage when a struggle involves significant elements of destructive conflict—conflict so extreme that it interferes with the mission of the organization. When a conflict intensifies, perceptions can become significantly distorted. Everyone convinces themselves that they are right and the other person is wrong.

In my research I examined a number of stories written by executive MBA candidates who were assigned to write a paper describing a major struggle episode. Looking over the stories, I counted the number of words the writers used to describe their own flaws and compared it with the number of words they used to describe flaws of others in the story.

I divided the data into two groups: cases where destructive conflict was prominent and cases where it was not. When there was no destructive conflict, the stories contained about an equal number of words describing self-failings and others' failings. But when destructive conflict was prominent, the stories portrayed the other party far more unfavorably. These results illustrate the dramatic distortions that can occur in people's perceptions of events during these types of episodes.

The conflict blind spot can cause someone to interpret every interaction through a distorted lens. Even if the other person did not intend any harm, the blind spot reinforces the perception that the other person is in the wrong, intensifying the emotions. This leads to further escalation, and the pattern becomes more ingrained. Issues become blown out of proportion, and emotions boil over.

To complicate matters further, conflict blind spots can blend with other blind spots, making them difficult to identify and address. Chapter 8 explores in greater detail destructive conflict and the problems created by the conflict blind spot.

⊘ EXPLORING PRACTICE

Overcome Your Blind Spots

Blind spots are different from other struggle scenarios we've examined so far. For one thing the effect of the blind spot may not show up immediately. Due to this time delay, you may not be aware that anything is amiss; you may not feel out of balance, and you may not even feel any tension. Thus you may miss the warning signs unless you pay careful attention. But then, seemingly out of nowhere, the situation can blow up, as it did for Joe Paterno more than 10 years after the initial Jerry Sandusky incident, or as it did for Dick Schulze four months after he confronted his company's CEO.

Become Aware of Blind Spots

By definition you are blind to your blind spots. That's why it's so important to proactively seek to discover them. It can be helpful to work with a coach who can systematically collect data for you by interviewing your boss, co-workers, and other colleagues. This rich qualitative data, especially when augmented by results of a personality test, can enable you to conduct your own analysis.

Take a look at your own past or current struggles and see if you can find any evidence of how your blind spots may have hindered your interactions and performance. You may also benefit by reviewing a different situation in your life when things didn't work out as you had hoped. Ask yourself what you can learn from it and what, if anything, you would do differently given the chance. If you find yourself writing about a conflict situation and focusing on the flaws of the other person, chances are your conflict blind spot is still active. Consider reframing the experience by looking at it from the other person's point of view. What flaws of yours would this other person see as major contributors to the conflict?

Still, your best efforts may fail to shine a light on your blind spots. There may be complex psychological mechanisms that trigger and perpetuate them. For example, by blaming the board for a faulty decision, Frank Russomanno's ego may have unconsciously protected him from directly reckoning with what the board saw as his CEO-related shortcomings. It took his wife's gentle, nonjudgmental questions to bring the blind spot to his conscious awareness so that he could deal with it in a healthy, productive way.

Even when someone has a vague awareness of a blind spot, psychological processes may keep the person anchored in safe, established patterns. It's possible that Joe Paterno felt some quiet discomfort at the thought of Jerry Sandusky's being in the presence of young children, yet apparently it never reached the threshold in his conscience that would have compelled him to take bold action.

Strategic blind spots can be especially problematic because the faulty assumptions they support can propagate unchallenged among an entire group. Consequently, people within the group tend to lose their objectivity, highlighting the need for dialogue and feedback from those outside the group. It may also be wise to carefully analyze the group's incentive systems, both implicit and explicit, to determine whether they are producing unwanted and unanticipated behaviors.

Be Your Own Change Agent: Conduct Mini-Experiments

Preventing blind spots from undermining your leadership requires rigorous, continuous discipline. Awareness is the first step, but the best leaders learn how to become their own change agent. It is all too easy to blame others or to coast along in comfortable yet unproductive patterns. It is much more difficult to embark on a path of growth and self-discovery.

Put your increased awareness to the test by trying some mini-experiments. If you are currently struggling with a situation, consciously look for subtle cues that you may have previously missed. Or try changing your behavior and then gauge the effect on those around you. For example, if you've discovered that the crux of your personality blind spot is that you tend to avoid conflict, try being slightly more assertive the next time you disagree with someone. Each time you try something new or notice something that may have slipped by you before, you have taken one more step on the path to becoming a better leader.

Transcend Conflict

Every human being makes mistakes, but when
he has made a mistake, that man who remedies
the evil is no longer foolish and unhappy.

— Sophocles, *Antigone*

Stent Wars

Mike Berman was promoted to president of the Boston Scientific Corporation (BSC) Cardiology Division in the summer of 1995 at age 37, just as intracoronary stents were beginning to eclipse balloon catheters as the preferred treatment for certain forms of heart disease. BSC, while a leader in the interventional cardiology business, was behind the pack in stent technology. To leapfrog the competition, Berman fostered a relationship with an Israeli firm, Medinol, that had developed a promising yet untested stent technology. The companies signed a 10-year agreement in October 1995, calling for Medinol to supply the stents to BSC, which would use its distribution muscle to deliver the products worldwide. Berman explained his view of the partnership:

> We thought our interests were aligned 100 percent, where they would make the stents, and we would take the stents and marry them to our product, package them, sterilize them, and then sell them around the world. So we built the delivery system; they built the stent. We married the two. And we were in charge of sales and marketing. I thought it would be a brilliant strategic move.
>
> But within a matter of months of signing this partnership agreement, it became apparent to me that while our interests were

aligned on paper, the style and the behind-the-scenes stuff were not aligned at all and that this would be a very difficult partnership for my people to work with. There was constant controversy, constant conflict, and constant disagreements—everything from how to sell, how to promote, how to price, and how to package, to what clinical trials to do, what sites to enroll in those clinical trials, and on and on and on. Everything was a flashpoint of conflict.

Ironically, in spite of the constant bickering, early financial metrics were very positive, and the innovative stent catapulted BSC to leadership in this fast-growing market. Still, the intense conflict was taking a toll. "It was grinding on everybody," Berman acknowledged. "Nobody was happy, including the Israeli partners."

One of the original contract stipulations required Medinol to assist BSC in building a backup manufacturing capability on BSC's premises. "The rationale behind this was that we wanted to make sure that if Medinol was not in a position to supply, for whatever reason, we would be able to supply our needs," Berman told me. "It seemed like Medinol would find every reason you can imagine—every excuse you can imagine—to not assist us in learning how to make stents."

By early 1997 Berman concluded that something needed to be done. He made a presentation to the board, recommending that BSC reexamine its relationship with Medinol, framing it as a "buy/bye" decision: either BSC should acquire Medinol or, if acquisition was not possible, move on and find some way to end the relationship.

Berman was a strong advocate for acquisition, believing that this was the only way to achieve 100 percent alignment of interests. With the board's blessing, he entered into discussions with Medinol, and by mid-1997 had arrived at a price that both he and Medinol felt was workable. The BSC CEO signed a term sheet, but a week later the deal fell apart. "The CFO felt like we were wasting $765 million," Berman explained. "His view was that Medinol was a captive company anyway. Why expend over $700 million because some people can't figure out how to make the relationship work?"

Often in conflict situations, there is a pivotal event that sows the seeds for things to come, setting in place a cascading chain of consequences that become increasingly difficult to reverse. It's possible that the 1997 breakdown in acquisition discussions was such an event.

Tensions escalated on myriad fronts, and, according to Berman, when Medinol continued its threats to cut off its supply of stents, BSC independently set up a backup stent manufacturing capability in Ireland, calling it Project Independence. Although BSC never actually used this plant to manufacture commercial product, it kept the existence of the facility a secret from Medinol.

Meanwhile, BSC's coronary stent market share in the United States, which had reached a high of 39 percent, started to erode. As competitors moved more quickly into the new drug-coated stent market, BSC remained enmeshed in conflict with Medinol.

In 1999 BSC had a new CEO, who by early 2000 decided to attempt a fresh start. Berman stepped aside so that the CEO could manage the relationship himself, and Berman, although offered another position, decided to leave the company. The new CEO paid Medinol more than $50 million in disputed fees, came clean on the facility in Ireland, and also proposed a possible acquisition of Medinol for $1.75 billion.

For a short time, it looked like the acquisition would go through. Then Medinol suddenly and unexpectedly broke off acquisition talks and filed a lawsuit seeking up to $4.6 billion in damages, claiming that it had been betrayed by BSC's surreptitious construction of the manufacturing capability. A brutal and protracted legal battle ensued, which was not resolved until September 2005, nearly 10 years after the original partnership deal was signed, when the two parties arrived at a negotiated settlement. BSC paid Medinol $750 million to end the contract, a fraction of the $1.75 billion Medinol had previously turned down.

When I interviewed Berman, he had long since moved past this time in his life. After leaving BSC he built a successful venture capital business, and he enjoys the respect of his community. He looked back with mixed emotions. On one hand he had built the BSC Cardiology business from $300 million to $1.5 billion in five short years and had more than 4,000 people working for him. On the other hand, there was a certain sadness and disappointment: "In all my years of work, there was really only one thing that I lost sleep over, and that was this relationship. And it was because it was so rife with conflict, so irrational. Here we were building a great business, and yet at the same time we had all this conflict and angst surrounding it. I had people reporting to me who were on the verge of nervous breakdowns because there was so much pressure on them."

Destructive Conflict

A certain amount of conflict can be healthy, especially in an atmosphere of trust. Diverse viewpoints can be expressed. Challenges to the status quo can push learning and innovation. Issues can be debated openly, often leading to better solutions. The trouble comes when the energy driving the conflict moves from positive and productive to negative and counterproductive. Conflict can then become destructive, often with disabling effects, undermining the very objectives to which the participants aspire.

One of the hallmarks of destructive conflict is a breakdown of trust, an essential ingredient in healthy relationships. Trust creates an atmosphere for people to safely explore their differences, leaving open the possibility that, collaboratively, they might arrive at a solution better than either of them could have imagined themselves. In a trusting environment, every human interaction, even when it involves disagreement, can be nourishing and fulfilling. But when trust erodes, all the positive elements of conflict are jeopardized. Collaboration evaporates, replaced by the fog of cynicism, anger, and hostility.

While the precise details of what transpired between BSC and Medinol are unknown, clearly there was an absence of trust in the relationship. The values of both companies were neither expressly articulated nor driving the pursuit of mutual goals. Somehow communication had broken down; perhaps key players had different expectations and assumptions. Whatever the reasons were—and likely there were many on both sides—the people involved retreated into secrecy and suspicion. Instead of becoming partners, they became enemies, obstinately locking horns in a destructive conflict.

Given the right circumstances, virtually anyone can fall prey to the conflict blind spot. Before either party realizes what's happening, destructive conflict can take on a life of its own. Patterns form that become self-reinforcing when one party negatively interprets the actions of the other party to fit unflattering preconceived notions.

Insight, empathy, and understanding fall by the wayside when the mind automatically filters all incoming data to prove what it already knows: the other person is wrong. Both sides become impervious to creative solutions that might be obvious to an objective observer. When the subtext of every interaction is about negotiating power rather than working together to create a win-win solution, transparency and teamwork become casualties.

Destructive conflict can occur between a boss and a subordinate, colleagues within a team, two departments or business units within a company, or business partners, as was the case with BSC and Medinol. The power dynamics can vary greatly, depending on circumstances. The ordeal usually takes a tremendous toll, sapping energy that could be more creatively and constructively invested in the project and its greater mission—as in the BSC story—and often inflicting lasting damage to the organizations and the individuals involved.

The deep feelings of distrust in destructive conflict are often accompanied by fears of diminished power. Motivations for every idea and action are called into question. Such a toxic environment does not support the high energy, creativity, and synergy that participants would ordinarily strive to bring to their projects. But we live in an imperfect world, and acknowledgment that we live in *the world as it is* is foundational to recognizing the potential for growth in any situation, even in the midst of destructive conflict.

Seeing through the Struggle Lens

At the core of struggle is a quality fundamental to the human condition: the tendency to strive to create something better than what currently exists. This yearning runs deep within us, enlivening our passions yet leaving us vulnerable to fixating solely on our own vision, losing sight of the fact that others may have different but equally legitimate visions.

Human struggles, even when taken on willingly, necessitate the abandonment of the old and the familiar in exchange for the hope and the promise of something new, different, and better. In conflict situations the parties involved bring different understandings and assumptions about how these transitions should be conducted—which articles of the past should be preserved or relinquished and which values should be emphasized in the future.

By examining a struggle narrative through the Struggle Lens, new pathways emerge for understanding and managing conflict. As the Struggle Lens states: *Leadership is a struggle by flawed human beings to make some important human values real and effective in the world as it is.* Three particular words—*flawed human beings*—are key to reaching a better understanding of the face of human conflict.

Among some of the leaders I interviewed, the declaration that human beings are flawed was a controversial premise. They openly questioned the relevance of this concept in a view of leadership, dismissing it as overly negative. But explicit acknowledgment that we are all flawed is necessary and important in our current times, when human perfection is put on a pedestal and often spuriously held up as a realistic goal. It is through greater awareness and acceptance of our own frailties that we open ourselves up to the potential for greater compassion, empathy, forgiveness, and understanding of others when conflict arises.

In an atmosphere of mistrust, the very air can seem toxic. Pleasantries become disingenuous or are discarded altogether, clearing the way for negative thoughts and emotions to surface. Fueled by suspicion, people become hypervigilant; they fear that they are being taken advantage of and that their dignity and sense of fairness may be under attack. Instead of explicitly acknowledging and labeling their fears, they may displace them with other emotions like anger, hurt, disgust, or self-righteousness. They may also project their fears onto others through blame and accusations. These psychological coping mechanisms protect them from the painful process of examining the root emotions at the base of their fears; however, doing so also "protects" them from any growth that might occur had they done the hard work of inner exploration. The Struggle Lens helps bring these fears into the sunlight of self-awareness and transforms them into opportunities for learning and personal development.

Goals versus Values

It's instructive to note that the word *goal* is notably absent from the Struggle Lens. This omission is an open invitation to examine the intricate interconnections between goals and values. Leaders have typically been trained to assume that leadership and goals are inseparable, so the absence of goals was frustrating for some leaders I interviewed. But the Struggle Lens, while not invalidating the need for goals, calls our attention to something deeper and more basic to human striving: the actualization of important human values. This "values first" approach is important because goals that are not in sync with individual and organizational values inevitably lead to external *and* internal conflict.

This realization opens a window of opportunity for productive dialogue in times of conflict. Take, for example, Joe Dowling's story of struggle with the Abbey Theatre's board. If Dowling and the board had not been blinded by their energy-sapping conflict, they might have begun a mutually respectful conversation about their differing prioritization of values as the theater ran into financial difficulties. Perhaps they could have then reached a compromise that honored both Dowling's yearning for artistic excellence and the board's mandate to be fiscally responsible.

To explore nuanced differences in priorities is to acknowledge that it is impossible to make *all* important human values real and effective and that a choice must be made about which values carry the most weight. There is no universal answer of course, and different stakeholders often have varied perspectives. Exploring these differences through conversation and reflection becomes especially critical during times of conflict. Unfortunately, teamwork and mutual respect are too often shunted aside by self-justification and rationalization.

The Struggle Lens brings into focus yet another aspect of the goals-versus-values conversation: the time dimension of goals. Leaders are often so compelled by arbitrary timeframes that they overlook important signals when conflict arises. They rush to get things done, anxious to place checkmarks in as many boxes as possible without fully appreciating how their urgency may actually undermine the very values they cherish the most. In some cases, they may be better served by slowing things down and taking time to consider the full spectrum of long-term considerations.

Transcending Conflict through Compassion and Healing

Compassion and *healing* are not common terms in the leadership vocabulary, but it's crucial to keep in mind that the people you are in conflict with are flawed human beings like yourself, with insecurities, fears, and emotional and psychological wounds—all of which color the way they perceive other people, the world, and the nature of conflict itself. Honoring the human face of conflict is the first step toward resolving that conflict in the healthiest way possible.

What does that look like? It begins with drawing on your capacity for compassion toward yourself and others in recognition that every human being is in need of healing on some level.

Your own healing begins with honest self-reflection and the willingness to openly confront your fears and self-doubts. You will then be better equipped to determine the right balance of values to actualize over the long term. The challenge is to do all this without allowing short-term urgencies to distract you and throw you off balance, which is no small task. While fictional stories of redemption, compassion, and healing are plentiful, real-world stories of transcendence are hard to come by. That's why the story of Julie Summers is particularly remarkable.

Summers is the CEO of a nonprofit organization dedicated to helping single mothers and their children break the cycle of poverty. The organization, which had a successful track record of operating in a single location, planned to expand its services through a new facility in a nearby city—let's call it Tulipville. If successful, this second facility could be the stepping-stone to a major expansion program bringing needed services to single mothers and their children nationwide.

Summers, a thoughtful and well-respected leader, carefully crafted the expansion plans. Her supportive board had announced a major fund-raising campaign to finance the new initiative. Members of the Tulipville community had invited the agency in. Drawing on her extensive background as a community organizer, Summers orchestrated support from key constituency groups. In fact, everything seemed to be going just right. That is, until the agency made an offer to purchase the land in Tulipville.

Summers told me that the conflict "started as an opposition by a few people and was further exacerbated by a lawsuit by a small group against our program. It then went public and became racially infused, laden with misconceptions about our program and misperceptions about me as an individual."

Summers was taken aback by the outpouring of anger directed at her and her program. While she wasn't sure what caused the anger, she speculated that it might have had something to do with a situation that occurred a long time ago, when a different agency had implemented a project that ended up causing significant displacement for many families in the community. Many of those displaced children had grown up to become key members of the community.

> They had never been heard in a real way about the anger they felt as young kids, watching their parents be displaced, seeing the businesses that they enjoyed in the community being destroyed. All that anger that they had as kids I don't think had ever been let out.

> When it first happened, I emotionally felt like it was a personal affront. How could they not trust me? My whole mission in life is to help women and children and to be a good role model. It felt very personal. I felt misunderstood. I felt like people were not giving me the opportunity to tell my story because there were all these assumptions being made that I would hear about.

Summers's first instinct was to tap into her wealth of experience as a community organizer. *I've got to talk to all these influencers in the community,* she told herself. *I have to go and prove myself. These people are judging me and they are judging the organization. We are both misunderstood. I've gotta go and tell them what the truth is.*

Fortunately, before she acted she took a step back. Tapping into her capability for self-reflection and self-awareness, she realized that she was reacting personally even though the protestors knew nothing personal about her.

> As individuals we all have buttons to get pushed once in a while. And for me one of those buttons is a feeling of being misunderstood. My dad died when I was young, and I had a single mom

who raised me when I was going to school. There would be times when I would feel, *Does anybody care? Does anybody understand what my aspirations are?* And, yes, this is my personal bugaboo. When things started to go wrong, that is where I went. That was a familiar place.

In my youth and young adulthood, I would remind myself that even though I did not know what I was going to do with my life, I knew that whatever I did it would be something of value. I knew it would be something that I was put on earth to do. So when I feel weak or victimized, I remind myself that I've got a greater purpose here than to feel sorry for myself.

Through her self-talk and her compassion for the protestors, Summers took steps to get back into balance. After some thought, she came up with a creative and empowering strategy: instead of confronting her critics, she went to their churches and prayed with them.

I decided to start showing up at their worship services—to simply mingle with people, to introduce myself to them, and to share in their services. As a churchgoing person, that was fine with me. I didn't mind it at all. Frankly, I found it quite enjoyable.

It was certainly uncomfortable at times because everybody who would go to those churches were members, and then I would show up. But what would be really interesting was that when I showed up, there would be people there who I know who would then say, "Oh. Hi." I would get this welcome by some congregants, and that would leave the people who were in opposition to me scratching their heads and thinking *How do they know her?* and *What is she doing here?* And I didn't go just once; I would go several times over the course of the year.

I asked Summers what drove her to worship at their churches.

What drove me was that I knew that their congregations were important to them. And I knew that the values of their congregations were similar to the values of what I would be trying to achieve there. So I was trying to, just by my presence, connect the dots: "You guys are all about empowering people to be their best selves. That's what my agency is trying to do. And, by association, if I come to your church and am worshiping with you, let's say, 'Yes, amen, let's help people be their best selves. Let's be generous. Let's ask God for forgiveness. Let's recognize the humanity in all of us. Let's forgive people.'"

I wanted them to know that I was no different from them. And despite the fact that we were of different races and that I was representing an official organization and they were community members, at the end of the day we were all just people. And so I became a real person to them.

Of course, all this relationship building took considerable time. The project's original timetable was delayed by more than six months. But the healing that occurred during the informal gatherings helped spark a dialogue. Summers says that she never confronted any individuals about their anger. Instead they talked about practical issues.

When the citizens expressed concern that a surface parking lot would be unattractive, the agency agreed to build underground parking so the surface area could be used for more aesthetic purposes. Opponents were also upset that the agency's tax-free status would rob the community of valuable property tax revenue. In the spirit of partnership, the agency agreed to pay the full tax on the property.

Fortunately, Summers's board was highly supportive. After Summers brought them up-to-date on the various issues, the board agreed that the original timeline and budget were unrealistic under the current circumstances. After additional discussion the board adopted different objectives that did not compromise the core values of the agency.

In the end Summers's critics turned into supporters. The facility was built, and the agency has already begun replicating its success in a nationwide expansion program.

Heal Yourself from Conflict

When you're in a situation involving destructive conflict, you may feel like the person you're in conflict with somehow slipped your arms into a straitjacket and yanked it tight when you weren't looking. You not only feel like your hands are tied behind your back but like you've been deprived of your freedom and dignity and that no matter how loudly you shout, no one will pay any attention to you. You're desperate to break free and make your voice heard. That's how Julie Summers felt: she wanted to let the whole world know that she was a caring, dedicated human being who was being judged unfairly.

Of course sometimes the person you're upset with during a conflict may be yourself. Even if you're engaging with the world as though nothing were wrong, just beneath the surface you may feel disgusted with your own conduct. It's risky to ignore such emotions; in the heat of the moment, negative feelings like guilt and self-blame can be expressed through acts of aggression.

Even if the conflict occurred years ago, the mere recollection of it can dredge up unpleasant memories. After more than a decade, Mike Berman admitted he was still troubled by the BSC-Medinol conflict. Joe Dowling also looks back with regret about his bitter battles with the Abbey Theatre board.

Such feelings are normal and understandable, yet it is important to not let them take root and spread like weeds in the soil of your consciousness. Silencing the automatic mind and adopting a growth mindset enables you to see a way out of the thicket of negative thoughts and feelings and begin moving toward healing and wholeness.

There are many pathways for healing, some of which were mentioned in the context of centering the mind, body, and spirit in chapter 5. Some people find healing through organized religion. Others seek it through meditation or yoga. Still others find inner peace by reading uplifting stories of healing and forgiveness.

What's most important to remember is that you cannot heal a situation until you heal yourself. Before you can release any anger you feel toward others, you must first release any anger you feel toward yourself. That requires you to forgive yourself for anything you did in the past that is making you feel guilty or remorseful today. A good place to start is by getting in touch with your fears.

Reflective Exercise: Begin Healing

Take a moment to think about the struggle experience you've been writing about in your notebook. Ask yourself: *What fears does this episode bring up in me? What self-doubts?*

It is not easy to admit to fears, to name them, to say them out loud, and to write them down. Doing so requires great strength of character, so be sure to recognize the wisdom and self-awareness you've acquired to even get you to this point. Once you begin confronting your fears, you've taken a big step toward healing. Ask yourself this question: *What healing do I need today?*

The path to inner peace has many entry points. You can choose a guided healing meditation on YouTube or from my website at snyderleadership.com. You can visit your church, synagogue, mosque, or temple. You can venture out into the woods or find a comfortable place to sit near water. You may prefer to seek counsel from a trusted friend or adviser, or simply get a hug and acceptance from a loved one. Whatever you choose, do it with the intent of releasing your hurt and anger.

You may want to write about your healing experiences in your notebook. Were you able to release the emotions that were troubling you? What other emotions did you experience in the process? How did you feel after completing each activity?

If you cannot find a way to release your anger and hurt just now, that's okay. If your feelings are especially intense or if they have been building for a while, it may be unrealistic to expect to release them all right away. Be patient and compassionate with yourself and continue to do your best. When you are ready, you will know it.

⊕ EXPLORING PRACTICE

Envision the Common Ground

Beginning the healing process creates space for new ways of looking at and dealing with conflict. The more compassionate and caring you become, the easier it will be to envision common ground with whomever you are in conflict with. Sometimes it is a common organizational mission that bonds you together. Other times, especially in the case of external partnerships, the connection may come from shared interests.

When the conflict stems not from an individual but from a group of some sort, it's important to remind yourself that groups are not faceless bureaucracies. All groups, no matter how much trouble you may have with them, are composed of unique individuals. Try to envision your relationship with each person separately. The more you can train yourself to look into individual faces and empathize with the position the people are in and where they may be coming from, the less likely you will allow yourself to become embroiled in destructive conflict.

Reflective Exercise: Envision Common Ground

If you currently find yourself in conflict with somebody, challenge yourself to envision the common ground the two of you share. Keep going until you gain clarity.

When you think about your colleague and the bond that connects the two of you, you may discover that his or her passion for the cause that unites you equals your own. That passion may just be expressed in a different way or through the filter of different priorities.

With this new understanding, you may begin to have more respect for your colleague and others with whom you have conflict. You may see them as flawed human beings, just like you, who are struggling to do the best that they can.

If you still see your colleague as the enemy, you may want to return to the exercise in "Exploring Practice: Heal Yourself from Conflict." Perhaps deeper self-healing is needed.

Next try to view your colleague as a flawed human being just like you who is worthy of your kindness and respect. Don't allow yourself to fall into the easy trap of doing so in a condescending way that elevates you above the other person. Instead strive to take on Julie Summers's understanding that "We are all just people" and that you and your colleague are far more alike than different in all the ways that really count.

In the previous exercise, you sought self-forgiveness; now it is time to forgive and accept your colleague as well. It is not necessary—and it may even be counterproductive—to directly communicate this acceptance to your colleague, who may not be in the same mental space that you are in. In fact, it is possible that he or she might never be in that space. That's okay because forgiveness is actually a gift you give to yourself.

Still the acceptance of your colleague as a fellow human being with whom you have a shared purpose eases the relationship tension between you. After all, if you improve your half of the relationship by remaining kind and compassionate, the whole relationship cannot help but improve. From a practical standpoint, because your changed attitude influences your behavior, you may even stop doing the things that antagonize your colleague.

With a new attitude and renewed focus, you are now ready to rebuild trust and forge a new relationship based on advancing your shared interests. One way to restore trust is with small gestures that show respect. Keep in mind that it might take a while for your colleague to even notice that you're being kind and respectful; in fact, if your colleague does notice it, he or she may not trust it at first. Just because you've had an epiphany doesn't mean that other people have changed. Your colleague is probably still marching forward with the same conflict blind spot, so you may need to exercise some patience. If you want to start the relationship anew but feel unsure about how to do it, you may consider seeking some guidance from a mentor, coach, or trusted friend.

When you manage to transcend your conflict blind spot and arrive at a more understanding, compassionate place, you will likely see pathways and solutions you had not seen before. This new vision makes it possible for you to put aside any differences that remain and concentrate on the interests that you and your colleague have in common.

If something in this exercise still doesn't feel quite right, it's possible that your inner voice is steering you in a different direction. It might be helpful to stop and pay attention, deciphering the message that could be hidden beneath the surface. Sometimes compromise isn't the best path, and part of the art of struggle is knowing when to stand up for what you feel is right, even if others disapprove. Chapter 9 explores those difficult choices.

9

Discover Purpose and Meaning through Struggle

Even when you think you have your life all mapped out, things happen that shape your destiny in ways you might never have imagined.

— Deepak Chopra, *The Spontaneous Fulfillment of Desire*

Difficult Choices

In the previous chapter, Mike Berman, president of Boston Scientific Corporation's Cardiology Division, became concerned about escalating conflict with a business partner. Early on Berman concluded that the only way to solve the problem was for BSC to acquire the company, thereby completely aligning the business interests of the two parties. With the board's blessing, Berman negotiated the acquisition deal, and a term sheet was signed by BSC's CEO. At the last minute, BSC's CFO intervened, nixing the deal.

When I asked Berman what he would have done differently if he had it to do over again, he pointed to this critical juncture. He wished that he had done more to win over the CFO to his point of view. He knew in his heart that an acquisition was the best path, yet he stood by and let the deal slip through his fingers, setting the stage for an ugly acceleration of tension and discord. Berman's choice would define his leadership; instead of doing battle with the CFO, in the end he opted to be a team player and go along.

Many of the stories you've read so far have involved important and sometimes difficult choices on a range of issues. Some leaders have taken bold stands, as Joe Dowling did when he abruptly and confrontationally resigned from the Abbey Theatre after the board wouldn't back down on an important issue. Others have made dramatic career moves, as Sandy Jones did when she gave up her dream of becoming chief merchant of a major retailer to pursue a career in helping people achieve health and well-being.

In this chapter these agonizing yet critical choices come squarely into focus. The stories of David Abelson, Ken Melrose, David Durenberger, Mark Sheffert, and Dick Schulze raise a number of issues that put leaders to the test:

- Deciding whether to take on a new opportunity that will help advance your career but that also carries significant risk

- Keeping yourself motivated and engaged when doing work that is difficult, unpleasant, or perhaps even in conflict with your beliefs

- Making difficult ethical decisions that may place your career on the line

- Balancing work, family, and community

- Dealing with life events that force you to reshuffle your priorities

In *True North* Bill George writes about discerning the core values and principles that guide an authentic leadership journey—finding your True North. This chapter probes how these principles and values are shaped and molded through the crucible of adversity, triggering questions central to a leader's identity: *Who am I? What are my hopes and dreams? What have I been put on this earth to do?* Or, as the Struggle Lens suggests, *Which of the many important human values do I wish to make real and effective through my leadership?*

In the midst of imperfect and flawed institutions in "the world as it is," actualizing important human values is no easy feat. It means coming to grips with the dialectical tension that erupts when lofty ideals clash with the practicalities of the real world. Yet by fully tapping that force inside you—your adaptive energy—you forge a synthesis, putting you more in touch with those things that fill your life with meaning and purpose. Whether it's a quiet whisper or a thunderous roar, you are more tuned in to the inner voice that steers you in the right direction.

A Quiet Voice

David Abelson, MD, has lived through many changes in both the practice and the business of medicine. Recognizing the opportunities offered by electronic medical information systems earlier than most, Dr. Abelson advanced into a position as chief medical information officer of a nonprofit, integrated health-care delivery system with more than 8,000 employees and revenues approaching $1 billion.

One day the CEO approached Dr. Abelson and asked if he would be willing to serve as interim CEO should anything happen to the current CEO. Dr. Abelson agreed but dismissed it as a low-probability event. Several months later, the CEO stepped up his recruiting efforts, wanting to build Dr. Abelson into a formal succession plan as the organization's next CEO. Taken aback, Dr. Abelson balked at the offer, telling the CEO no several times.

Soon after, Dr. Abelson had a change of heart. He told me: "This may sound corny, but at some point I finally acknowledged that there was a very quiet voice inside of me that said, 'You could bring a lot of value by being CEO.' It probably took me several months to acknowledge to myself that I had been hearing it for a while, and there was actually some internal resistance on my part to even acknowledging that the voice was there."

I asked Dr. Abelson what was keeping him from acknowledging the voice. He replied: "I was actually very comfortable in what I was doing. And I knew that it would be a struggle to lead an organization with all the uncertainties in my mind. I also knew that CEOs often don't last very long."

Dr. Abelson finally consented, allowing his name to be placed on the succession plan. I asked him what made him change his mind. "It was not an aha! moment," he said. "There was a very gentle whisper that just got a little louder. Finally, I asked myself, *What's this about, David?* That was transformative, to admit that I heard that voice. It was not that I wanted more power or authority. At some point I just heard an internal voice saying that being CEO would be my way of bringing value. It was almost a sense of reverence."

Twelve months later, just as the financial crisis of 2008 was getting into full swing, the succession plan was implemented and Dr. Abelson became the CEO. It was difficult, as he had predicted, but he feels he made the right choice by listening to his quiet voice as it got louder.

I reconnected with Dr. Abelson a year after my initial interview to ask him how things were going. He told me: "I consider leadership 'an inward journey to outwardly serve.' The inward journey relates to bumping into my own limits and fears with each leadership challenge. Will I have the courage for the difficult conversations? Will I be able to separate my self-interests and biases from the best leadership practice? To paraphrase T. S. Eliot, 'Leadership requires stillness to hear our quiet voice between two waves of the sea.'"

Why Am I Here?

Like Dr. Abelson, Ken Melrose hadn't planned to lead an organization during a time of crisis. At 40 he became CEO of Toro Company, the lawn care giant, as it teetered on the edge of bankruptcy. He was charged with guiding the company through a change of epic proportions—shedding 2,400 employees representing 60 percent of the workforce. Melrose told me what was going through his mind at the time:

> I was ill prepared for the job. How do I lead through this morass? I just abhorred the idea of coming into work and having to sit down with a group of people reporting to me and decide the fate of this plant, this department, and then to go to them and say, "We are shutting this part of the business down. You've lost your job." My background was marketing, which meant caring for customers. It meant growing the company, finding ways to build. And now I was in a position where I had to unbuild and dismantle.

The most difficult thing for Melrose was laying off people who had become his friends.

> Some employees would cry, men as well as women. And I would be sitting there feeling just terrible about it, about myself, and about what I was doing. It was a depressing period of time. I felt lost. Who could I go to? I was the boss. I couldn't go to my boss and say, "I don't like doing this. Can you get somebody else to do it?" The buck stopped at my desk, as they say.

> Somebody said, "Well, you are really not alone in this." And I said, "I don't see anybody else above me whom I can complain to." And that person said, "Well, what about God?" I said, "You're right. I'm not in this alone." From then on, if I were feeling kind of low after terminating someone or making a difficult decision affecting others, I would think, *God is with me. This is going to be okay.*

Onward to the Senate

In 1978 David Durenberger faced a series of difficult choices. Successful in his corporate job, he was also serving on a number of state boards and commissions. His contributions to Minnesota as a private citizen were significant, but he felt he could do more by becoming a change agent in the political arena. After he decided to leave his job to run for governor, a position for which he felt qualified, Republican leaders endorsed another candidate. The GOP did, however, encourage him to run for the US Senate and pledged their support if he would do so.

Durenberger had spent several years as chief of staff for a Minnesota governor before transitioning to corporate life, so he was familiar with a governor's responsibilities. But he was completely unfamiliar with a senator's duties and responsibilities, not to mention the accompanying lifestyle changes that would come with the position.

"I went to Washington and talked to people who had been governors who were then in the Senate," he told me. "Each of them asked me, 'Why were you running for governor?' I said, 'Because I want to change the role of government.' They said, 'Well, you've got to go where all the money is, and all the money is going to Washington. That's the only way you are going to change things.'"

Despite this encouragement Durenberger still had strong concerns on the personal front. Moving to Washington, DC, would be a tremendous upheaval for him and his family. His first wife had died, leaving him with four young sons. Although he had remarried, he was seriously concerned about the impact such a move would have on his children, who were likely still grieving the loss of their mother.

Durenberger weighed going back to his corporate job; he had been happy there, and it paid well. At the same time, he honestly felt he could make a difference in Washington. It was an agonizing decision, but in the end he relied on his Catholic faith to guide him. He accepted his party's call and was elected to the US Senate.

For the next decade, Durenberger was a highly respected and valued member of the Senate, where he served as Minnesota's voice on energy, tax, and health-care policy. Then, in 1990, after nearly two years of investigation, Durenberger was charged with ethics violations for financial misconduct and was censured by the Senate. He served the remaining four years of his term under a cloud.

Durenberger acknowledged at the time of his censure that his "judgment was impaired"; he apologized for his errors, accepted full responsibility for them, and asked his Senate colleagues for their forgiveness. As before, Durenberger turned to his faith to help him through a difficult time: "The act of real contrition that goes with that loving relationship combined with forgiveness creates a whole new strength to avoid falling in that trap a second time. For me it's a way to convert your sins into a positive. So I acknowledge that in everything I do and in every part of my life."

Durenberger, whom I view as a good, well-intentioned man who briefly lost his way due to his financial struggles, stressed to me his own sincere contrition for his actions and added that recognition of his own flaws and mistakes made him more willing to forgive others.

Back home in Minnesota, a more humble Durenberger, who considers himself a better person for having gone through the ordeal, has regained his stature as a nationally respected voice for Minnesotans and an authority on one of the country's thorniest issues: health-care policy and strategy.

A Matter of Integrity

At 40 Mark Sheffert was promoted to CEO of the Trust Division of a large bank. A rising star at the bank, he had amassed an impressive set of accomplishments that led the bank to put him in charge of a delicate and complex situation: the bank's computer systems had suffered a meltdown, causing errors on many 401(k) statements the bank had prepared for employees of its large corporate clients.

Sheffert was faced with two options: He could openly admit the problem to the bank's corporate clients, shut down the system for three months for repairs, and then reissue the statements with the correct information. Another option was to continue with the current system until a fix was available and then quietly slide in the changes without any fanfare.

The stakes were high. A system shutdown could cause clients to abandon the bank, placing a large recurring revenue stream in jeopardy. A significant deviation from planned earnings could put Sheffert's career in jeopardy, as well. On the other hand, keeping quiet had its own risks. The system would continue to produce erroneous data for several more months. The sales force would need to keep customer questions and concerns at bay, providing evasive answers that did not reveal the core truth of the situation.

When Sheffert learned that some board members and senior company leaders favored the quiet route, he did some intense soul searching. Could he proceed down this path while preserving his integrity? He would know the truth. His people would know the truth. What implications would this course of action have for him and his organization?

> I had always operated with a high degree of ethics, and I totally believe in being open and transparent. But given the magnitude of those various struggles, it did cause me to sit back and think, *Gee, maybe we could do this.* You begin to play mind games with yourself, and you start to rationalize unethical behavior.
>
> But I had three problems. One is, when I get up in the morning to shave, I don't like sneaking up on the mirror one cheek at a time. I didn't want to be ashamed of myself. Second, the employees would know that we were being dishonest. How are they going to respect me as a leader if they see that I am a party to a scheme to misrepresent our position to customers? And, third, I had a board of directors whom I answered to and who I believed expected me to be an honest, ethical person.
>
> At the end of the day, I finally concluded that even though the second option may have been emotionally and financially easier, it wasn't worth it. What I may have gained in profit, I would have lost in psyche.

Sheffert convinced his board to go with the transparency strategy. He personally visited the CEOs of all of his large clients to explain the situation. He told them what had happened and what the bank was doing about it. He humbly asked for their patience and promised that the problem would be fixed within several months.

The strategy worked. The bank lost very few clients. More importantly, Sheffert felt he had made this difficult decision with integrity. Convinced it was the right choice, he boldly moved forward, trusting that everything would work out in the end.

While some may be surprised that Sheffert even considered not disclosing the problem, his dilemma illustrates that even good leaders can drift toward rationalizing away unethical choices. What distinguishes the best leaders is that they don't act on those rationalizations. Integrity is not relative—you either have it or you don't—but the higher the stakes, the more tempting it can be to at least consider options that appear to be less painful than doing the right thing.

Sheffert's dilemma also illustrates the importance of standing firm on your integrity despite pressures you might feel from those with more power. By independently coming to his own conclusion and then guiding his board to support him, Sheffert defined himself as a leader, making real and effective those values and principles that before were just theoretical and abstract.

Dick Schulze

Work and Family Balance

Work and family balance come into play in many stories of leadership struggle. Every day can bring with it difficult choices. Should you go home to have dinner with your family or stay late at the office to better prepare for the next day's presentation or meeting? Should you respond to that troubling e-mail you got over the weekend or ignore it and be in the right frame of mind for your daughter's swim competition?

Ultimately, you need to decide how much energy you want to devote to building your career and your organization and how much time you want to spend with your family and friends and serving the larger community. This time-allocation decision may require adjustments throughout your career, depending on your stage of life and the unique circumstances at hand.

Dick Schulze, founder and former chair and CEO of Best Buy, learned this the hard way. He told me of his single-minded commitment to grow the company at the expense of time with his family. His wife, Sandra, was extraordinarily supportive. "She would defer any and all of her own priorities to mine," he said. "She supported me through thick and thin in everything I chose to do."

Schulze had promised Sandra that he would retire at age 62. "I said I was going to get out of the active flow of the business, and we were going to spend the rest of our lives enjoying the fruits of our labor," he told me.

Tragically, Sandra was diagnosed with mesothelioma, a rare form of cancer, several years before Schulze reached his planned retirement age. He dropped everything to be at his wife's side and devoted all of his time to her until she died. But their dreams of traveling and spending their retirement years together were never realized.

When I interviewed him in 2011, Schulze had remarried and his priorities had changed. After retiring as CEO of Best Buy, he moved to Florida, where he could spend more time with his new wife and friends. His focus had shifted away from Best Buy to philanthropic causes, most notably seeking a cure for type 1 diabetes. Then, in May 2012, the Brian Dunn incident surfaced and everything changed.

To the Rescue

Recall from chapter 7 that Schulze was forced to resign as chair of the company he had founded. Soon he would also announce his resignation from the board. Almost immediately, rumors began circulating that Schulze would attempt to take back control of the company in a leveraged-buyout effort.

I talked to Schulze in early July 2012, about three weeks before his buyout plan was publicly announced. He told me of his growing frustration with the Best Buy board. He felt that the company was not acting aggressively enough to confront the challenges of a new business climate that was highlighted by growing web-based competition from Amazon. This frustration had been building for some time, and the Dunn ordeal was the catalyst that brought things to a head.

Although Schulze could not yet talk openly about the buyout plans, the excitement came through in his voice as he told me, "I haven't felt this jazzed since 1983." Schulze was referring to the time when he rescued his failing company, Sound of Music, and led it through the transformation that created what we now know as Best Buy.

Schulze has a lot riding on the outcome. His 20 percent ownership stake had fallen in value as Best Buy's stock price plummeted. Things took a dramatic turn in mid-August when negotiations between Schulze and Best Buy's board broke down and Best Buy announced that it had hired a new CEO. Discussions have since resumed, but at the time of this writing the dance has not ended, and many questions remain. Can Schulze successfully engineer the buyout? Will the distraction caused by Schulze's bid further hobble an already weak company? And if Schulze prevails with the buyout bid, will he be able to turn the company around? Or will the additional debt taken on through a leveraged buyout sink the whole ship? Then again, what about the wildcard of the new Best Buy CEO, Hubert Joly? Will he introduce something new and completely unexpected into the mix?

One thing is clear: at 71 years old, Schulze has entered a new phase of life. Emerging from his struggle, he made the choice to again refocus his energies—this time centered on rescuing and restoring to health the company he founded 46 years earlier.

Courage Tempered with Humility

The stories in this chapter illustrate the importance of balancing courage with humility when making difficult choices. Only through bold, courageous action did David Abelson, Ken Melrose, and Mark Sheffert realize their full potential as leaders, dramatically resolving tensions of identity in the moment of truth.

Yet at the same time, there is a need for caution and humility—caution about weighing the risks involved and humility to accept the consequences of those risks when they don't play out in your favor. Despite careful calculations and planning, one often has no way to know in advance how risky a decision might be. David Durenberger did extensive due diligence before agreeing to run for the Senate, yet he failed to fully anticipate the economic consequences of his decision.

Over time, through accumulating experience and diligently pursuing a growth mind-set, you will enable your intuition to guide you with greater foresight and accuracy.

Reflective Exercise: Ask Yourself Some Hard Questions

The choices you make—large and small—are the most vivid expression of your leadership. They reflect who you are as a person. It's one thing to talk about your values, but through the actions you take and the choices you make, they become visible for the whole world to see.

This reflective exercise and the two practices that follow are among the most important in this book, inviting you to address the most fundamental of questions. You may wish to write your answers in your notebook or reflect on them in the stillness of meditation. Give yourself permission to tap into any tensions of identity that may be brewing under the surface, and feel free to write questions of your own that more specifically address your unique circumstances.

- Do I feel energized by what I am currently doing in my career and in my life?

- Do I feel like what I am doing now gives my life meaning and purpose? What specific aspects of my work are the most meaningful? What important aspects are missing?

- Are there ethical issues that concern me?

■ Am I at the crossroads of an important decision? If so, what decision am I faced with and why? Are their implicit decisions that I am not yet seeing? What are they?

■ What changes do I want to make personally and professionally?

■ How will these changes help me find meaning and purpose in what I do?

■ What are my dreams for the future? How do I know that they are right for me?

Now might be a good time to revisit a couple of earlier questions:

■ What script am I playing out right now? Do I like it? Do I want to choose a different script?

■ What does my current tension map look like? Does it still look the same as when I first drew it? Has anything changed? Have I changed?

⚡ EXPLORING PRACTICE

Write or Revise Your Personal Vision Statement

You may already have a vision statement. If you do, find it and read it. You may even want to read it aloud so that you can hear the sounds of the words. Does it still feel right to you? Do your current circumstances suggest any changes?

If you do not yet have a written vision statement, imagine yourself in your seventies crafting one for the person you are today. Ask yourself: *What would I like to say about my life and about who I am as a human being by the time I reach my seventies?*

Imagining yourself looking back on your journey in this way can give you a fresh perspective, incorporating a decision-making heuristic that I first learned from Jeff Bezos. He calls it the "Principle of Least Regret." In essence it asks: If you were 70 years old and looking back on your life, which of the paths you are currently considering would you least regret taking?

After you complete your draft or revision, you may want to meditate on what you came up with, or perhaps read it aloud and see if it feels right to you. It's a good sign if you feel reenergized and like you're heading in the right direction.

It's now time to apply your future dreams to your current circumstances.

⊕ EXPLORING PRACTICE

Recommit, Pivot, or Leap

With your vision clearly articulated, you are better equipped to assess how well your current activities are aligned with that vision. You can start by taking another look at the hard questions you asked yourself earlier in this chapter: *Do I feel energized by what I am doing in my career and in my life? Does it fill me with meaning and purpose? What's keeping it from being satisfying?*

Now take it one step further. Ask yourself, *Am I willing to rededicate myself to my current endeavors, or do I need to segue to something new? And if I do choose a new route, what should it be?*

Essentially, you have three options: The first is to recommit to your current direction. The second is to *pivot,* or make a midcourse correction. It's a term often used in sports; with one foot planted firmly on the ground, you move the other foot in a different direction, altering your trajectory. The third option is to make a more dramatic leap, perhaps into a totally new arena, far beyond the comfort zone of your previous experiences.

In the stories presented in this book, you can see that different leaders made different decisions. Ken Melrose opted to recommit. After confronting his struggle, he realized he was in exactly the right place. Even though it pained him at times, he did his best to efficiently resize the company so that it could remain viable.

David Abelson and Joe Kelly made pivots. Heeding his inner voice, Dr. Abelson agreed to be considered for the CEO position. Captain Kelly changed branches, although he remained in the army. Both of these decisions involved altering direction while maintaining a link to past experience.

David Durenberger, Sandy Jones, Joe Dowling, and Dick Schulze took leaps of varying proportions. Durenberger moved into the unknown waters of the Senate. Jones moved from a career in merchandizing to helping others live healthier and more balanced lives. Dowling bolted from the Abbey Theatre without the safety net of a new job. With the leveraged buyout, Schulze is attempting perhaps the biggest leap of all. Even though it involves a company he knows intimately, Schulze's bold actions have sent both him and Best Buy into uncharted territory, generating both opportunity and uncertainty.

These options—recommit, pivot, or leap—all carry different risk profiles. Only you can decide which one best suits your situation, given your economic circumstances, your family responsibilities, your stage of life, your hopes and dreams, and your tolerance for risk.

You may need to gather more data before making your decision. For example, the questions presented here may prompt you to initiate a new dialogue with your employer to explore whether your current role can be adapted to better suit your personal and professional aspirations. Respectful dialogue will likely give you a better understanding of the organizational viewpoint; it may also give you an opportunity to influence the organization's direction. Your support network might prove helpful by offering you honest, caring feedback.

If you decide to stay where you are, don't allow yourself to coast; actively recommit with the intention to fully engage. The process of recommitting will put you in a different psychological state that may supply you with added motivation and a broader perspective. If you find yourself hesitating about recommitting, you can time-bound your commitment: plunge into your job with renewed focus but reevaluate your status in 12 to 18 months. By giving the strategies you've learned in this book a chance to work, you may be surprised to find that the limits you once perceived to be holding you back have dispersed, leaving space for you to grow, develop, and contribute more than you previously imagined possible.

In part II you've explored multiple new pathways, with the goal of gathering and deploying your adaptive energy in the most effective ways possible. You've met leaders who reimagined their situations to discover new alternatives. Others reinvented themselves to adapt to challenging circumstances. You've seen leaders who overcame their blind spots and some who did not. You've witnessed the devastating power of destructive conflict and learned how the Struggle Lens can invigorate your perspective. In this chapter you've pondered some tough questions and hopefully have achieved a new level of awareness about your purpose and direction, emerging with a new sense of energy and commitment.

In the third and final part of this book, you will further deepen your understanding of adaptive energy. By turning this page, you will begin your exploration of how to link your current circumstances to the future you see when you close your eyes and dare to dream.

Part III

Deepening Adaptive Energy

DEEPENING PRACTICES

Prepare for What Lies Ahead

Harness the Engine of Discipline

Celebrate What's Precious

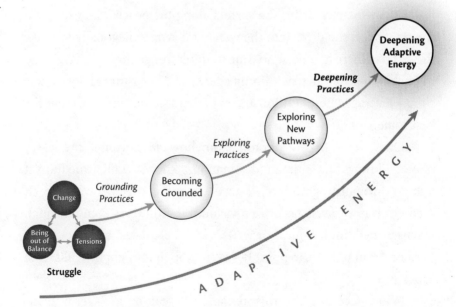

10

Peer into the Future

A rock pile ceases to be a rock pile the moment a single mind contemplates it, bearing within him the image of a cathedral.

— Antoine de Saint-Exupéry, *Flight to Arras*

THROUGHOUT HIS CAREER, RICHARD FEYNMAN, A CO-WINNER OF the 1965 Nobel Prize in physics, remained fascinated by a simple observation: No matter which medium a photon of light passes through, it always chooses the fastest path to arrive at its destination.

Consider the analogy of a lifeguard who spots someone in trouble 200 feet to her left and 100 feet from shore. Knowing she can run faster than she can swim, she sprints along the beach. Choosing just the right spot, she dives into the water and swims diagonally to make the rescue. There had been no time to think things through. Factoring in her destination, her swimming speed, and her running speed, she simply leveraged her intuition and experience to instantly map out the best route.

Okay, back to the photon. Somehow, *in advance,* the savvy photon "knows" its ultimate destination, "knows" which medium it will go through to get there, "knows" how fast it can travel in each medium (light travels faster in a vacuum than it does going through a denser medium like glass or water), and "calculates" the fastest way to move from point A to point B—even though it might be trillions of miles away.

What accounts for this remarkable feat of long-term planning? Feynman theorized that the photon somehow taps into a yet undiscovered link between the present and the future to determine the fastest path.

Like photons and lifeguards, good leaders learn to intuit the link between their current circumstances and future potentialities. They develop the capacity to supplement logic and reason with the intuitive ability to synthesize an almost endless array of variables to anticipate what the future might hold. This capacity for intuitive analysis is accessible to all of us. Through effort and experience, you can sharpen your intuition and become more adept at orchestrating the delicate dance between your automatic and reflective mental processes. As Steve Jobs said: "You can't connect the dots looking forward; you can only connect them looking backwards. You have to trust that the dots will somehow connect in your future. You have to trust in something— your gut, destiny, life, karma, whatever. Because believing that the dots will connect down the road will give you the confidence to follow your heart, even when it leads you off the well-worn path."

You can learn to anticipate and prepare for the future in several ways. You can envision opportunities—changes in markets, technology, or competition—that create windows for innovation and ingenuity. You can learn how to anticipate potential obstacles—constraints and pitfalls that could potentially derail your plans. You can nurture your adaptive energy by growing your skills and capabilities to tap into the full potential of what's ahead.

In 1984 during my tenure at Microsoft, I was fortunate enough to participate in a memorable executive retreat. I traveled with Bill Gates, Steve Ballmer, Paul Allen, John Shirley, and several others to a picturesque island hideaway to discuss the company's long-term strategy.

I vividly recall the moment when Bill spoke about an emerging capability made possible by the new media of compact discs (CDs). Back then audio CDs were just becoming popular, but Bill envisioned how the CD's digital capability could be extended to store 700 megabytes of data of any sort. I remember Bill glancing down at a CD in his hand while speculating about the new possibilities it promised, including the distribution of multimedia encyclopedias that would feature photos, sound clips, and even video. While such advanced technology seems quaint by today's standards, back then it was a quantum leap, given that the only way to disseminate information was through 1.2-megabyte floppy disks. A CD-ROM (compact disc–read-only memory) would represent a six-hundredfold increase in capacity.

If Bill's vision were to be realized, an entirely new industry would have to spring up. There needed to be a standard protocol for recording data onto a CD-ROM. Programmers would need new tools to create CD-ROM applications. CD-ROM readers would need to be installed on a critical mass of computers.

Then, of course, there was the question of how Microsoft should mobilize to be the catalyst for this exciting new technology. It would require a lot of smart, savvy people and significant investments of time, energy, and money. But it was Bill's vision that it *could* be done—and his articulating the path clearly enough so that others could under-stand and know what to do to make it happen—that made such a breakthrough possible.

Predictably, there were a number of obstacles that needed to be overcome before Bill's vision could come to fruition. Realizing your own vision requires that you be ever watchful for potential obstacles that could prevent you from crossing the goal line. These roadblocks may include blind spots, organizational challenges, market resistance, competitive responses, or personal adversity.

Mary Brainerd, the CEO of HealthPartners, the largest consumer-governed, nonprofit health care organization in the country, has learned that her optimistic outlook, normally a strength, can be a potential blind spot with respect to anticipating potential problems. Consequently, she taps into her collaborative leadership philosophy to engage her team in preparing for initiatives and major meetings. "Preparation is not a solo act," she told me. "When I think of really challenging decisions, situations, or meetings, I never feel as well prepared as when I prepare with others. We seldom do a key meeting or key session without a design session ahead of time."

Guerrero-Anderson's Intuition and Transformation

Leaders who develop a keen intuitive sense of how to prepare for their next stage in life are able to proactively reinvent themselves in anticipation of future challenges. Consider Esperanza Guerrero-Anderson, born in Managua, Nicaragua, whose father abandoned her and her mother two days after she was born. In the aftermath of this trauma, her mother taught her that she always needed to look out for herself first because she could not rely on others to take care of her. Guerrero-Anderson understandably internalized this value system. When she entered the working world, she valued money, status, and power above all else; those were her tickets to career advancement and ultimate security.

By age 30 Guerrero-Anderson had been working at the Central Bank of Nicaragua for several years. Her upward progression through traditional positions, however, appeared to be blocked by longstanding incumbents. When she became aware of an emerging opportunity in management information systems (MIS), a trend that was starting to revolutionize organizations in the 1970s, she convinced the bank to send her to study MIS in the United States.

Before starting her studies, she enrolled in an English-as-a-second-language course. As part of an exercise, the teacher asked the class, "What would your father have liked you to be." Guerrero-Anderson told me that most of the students, who had come from upwardly striving families, said things like, "My father would have liked me to be president . . . a congressman . . . Supreme Court justice . . . grandiose things."

> Then out of the blue, from the back of the class, a woman from Japan said, "My father would have liked me to be a good person." And that changed my life.

I had never heard that in my entire life. Or, if I heard it, I didn't listen. I never heard anybody say that they wanted to be a better human being—not success, power, achievement, or awards but to be a better human being.

Guerrero-Anderson internalized this new value system and completely reinvented herself as a leader. Instead of striving for power and money, she began striving to be a better human being. This transformation prepared her for even greater success when she returned to work in Nicaragua. Instead of focusing on her own success, she began focusing on how to help other people in the bank succeed. She became open and transparent.

It took a while for people to trust her. Her attitude was so different from everyone else's at the bank—and so different from what it had been before she left for the United States. But her new value system was exactly what was necessary to move the bank forward. It allowed her to introduce new ideas that involved information sharing and open collaboration among departments, something unheard of at a bank riddled with fiefdoms.

One challenge was finding the best people to staff the new MIS area. Historically, the bank's method for selection revolved around cronyism, where powerful executives would choose their friends or relatives for plum assignments. But in the United States, Guerrero-Anderson had learned of a better system based on aptitude testing, which would select the people who had the greatest chance of performing well. Through her earnest and honest approach, she was able to convince the bank's decision makers that everybody, as well as the bank itself, would be better off if the selection system for these vital new jobs was overhauled.

Guerrero-Anderson's influence continued to grow. In addition to heading MIS, she became responsible for human resources development—not only at the bank but for the entire country of Nicaragua. Then, in 1979, to escape the Sandinista revolution she fled to the

United States, where she continued to reinvent herself repeatedly over the next three decades.

Now it's your turn to put on your visionary cap. What steps will *you* take to prepare yourself to create *your* future?

♡ DEEPENING PRACTICE

Prepare for What Lies Ahead

*Envision What Your Industry Might
Look Like in Five or 10 Years*

Spending time with Bill Gates in his formative leadership years gave me a privileged perch for observation. It turns out that Bill's sagacity and insight do not stem solely from innate genius. He surrounds himself with very smart people, and he's a voracious reader. Every year he goes off for what he calls "think week." He takes a mountain of books (or nowadays, perhaps, an electronic book reader), pores through them, and sifts through the nuggets upon which he wants to act.

If you ever wanted to be more like Bill Gates, here's your opportunity. You too can become hyperinquisitive and actively seek out the thought leaders in your industry or field. Get yourself connected and inspired. Attend professional conferences or idea conferences, like TED or the Aspen Ideas Festival. If you can't go in person, search the web; a lot of great talks are available for free. Talk to smart people. Follow thought-provoking blogs. Read books. Read more books. Read even more books. Create your own vision for the future.

Prepare Yourself by Building the Skills You Will Need

It is not always easy to identify which skills will help you maximize your leadership potential. But one core leadership capability that is crucial to the theme of this book is emotional intelligence, which implies self-awareness, the maturity to manage your own emotional state, and the ability to notice social cues so as to maintain good relationships with others. Practicing mindfulness or participating in peer support groups like True North Groups (discussed in chapter 5) will help you build emotional intelligence as will working on your blind spots (as outlined in chapter 7). These approaches strengthen the power and the efficacy of the reflective processes that are so crucial to enlightened leadership. Recent scientific evidence suggests yet another pathway for building emotional intelligence and becoming a better leader: reading fiction.

This may sound surprising, but in a series of studies psychologists Raymond Mar and Keith Oatley found that readers of fiction were better able to understand their social world, feel more empathy for others, and more thoroughly comprehend the vantage point of another person. The narrative quality of fiction helps build an elaborate map in your brain, enabling you to better understand others' intentions. Essentially, the brain does not differentiate between an actual social experience and a simulated social experience through reading a narrative. So when you read stories, your brain naturally conducts multiple simulations, building an increasingly comprehensive model of why people behave the way they do.

This brain map provides more than just intellectual or theoretical understanding. Fiction—and literature more broadly—travels on a visceral and experiential plane. When you read a novel, biography, or memoir—or see a play or movie—you step outside yourself and enter new worlds to explore. These worlds feel bracingly real while you're immersed in them; you connect with the characters that inhabit them in your heart and your gut. Through the power of story, you come to know the soothing glow of compassion and forgiveness, the soul-cleansing capacity of healing and transcendence, and the nurturing warmth of tranquility and inner peace.

Literature also lends a portal into the moral world, providing a nuanced language to help you examine, tune, and sharpen your own sense of ethics and morality. It holds a mirror up in front of you and confronts you with challenging questions. Literature can help you develop character—the foundation of moral and ethical qualities that empowers you to live an honorable life.

In my conversations with leaders, I probed the connection between leadership and literature. Some told me of being inspired by classic novels such as Charles Dickens's *Great Expectations,* Leo Tolstoy's *Anna Karenina,* and Harper Lee's *To Kill a Mockingbird* or more-contemporary novels like Kathryn Stockett's *The Help.* Others pointed to fictionalized historical accounts like Michael Shaara's Pulitzer Prize–winning *Killer Angels.* Still others preferred biographies of great leaders like Winston Churchill and Abraham Lincoln. Mary Brainerd, the CEO of HealthPartners, mentioned a novel she had read just before our interview: Laurence Cossé's *A Novel Bookstore.* "It made me think differently about the values associated with 'good,'" she said. "Who picks 'good'? What does 'good' mean?"

Predictably, I had an enlivened conversation with Joe Dowling, artistic director of the Guthrie Theater, who by the nature of his job stands at the very crossroads of these two fields. He told me about one of his favorite plays, Shakespeare's *Julius Caesar,* and the lessons we can learn from the playwright's portrayal of its many flawed characters. Summing up the power of literature to shape leaders, Dowling said: "You cannot be a leader without being a student of the human condition. So if you want to know about how people live and what it is that makes the world go round, and what it is that drives people to make certain choices in their lives, you've got to read literature. You've got to read fiction. You've got to read poetry. You've got to see plays. You've got to see the cinema."

Steve Jobs famously showed a slide with the intersection of Liberal Arts and Technology Streets. I advocate for another street sign: the intersection of Leadership and Literature Avenues. Through literature we reinsert our humanity back into our leadership. So by all means pick up a few high-quality novels and enjoy some live theater whenever you can. Who would have guessed that meeting great characters can help you build great character?

11

Savor the Marathon

It was like hearing a piece of fabric woven with all
the colors of a rainbow. I did not know that such
beauty could be formed by the human mouth.

— Anita Diamant, *The Red Tent*

"Leadership is a marathon, not a sprint," an astute leader told
me. Like long-distance runners who take in nourishment along the
way, you need to continually nourish yourself, replenishing the energy
you've lost and sustaining yourself through life's difficulties, all the
while continuing your path of growth and mastery. Here are two final
suggestions to help you get the most out of your journey.

⬡ DEEPENING PRACTICE

Harness the Engine of Discipline

Transforming Old Habits into New Adaptive Patterns

Great leaders bring a high level of discipline to their roles and their lives.
This discipline manifests in the form of habits—behavioral routines
that play out over and over again. Typically, these routines produce
some kind of reward of which you may or may not be fully conscious.
The trick is to find just the right routine and just the right reward to
transform your habits into a self-perpetuating adaptive engine.

The process of struggle can transform old habits that may have
been adaptive in the past but are no longer so into new patterns that
connect more deeply with your aspirations and dreams. Randy Hogan,

the CEO of Pentair whom you met in chapter 6, exemplifies this transformative process.

Hogan spent two years in the US Coast Guard Academy before transferring to the Massachusetts Institute of Technology, where he earned a bachelor's degree in civil engineering. After working for several years, he returned to school to earn an MBA at the University of Texas at Austin. He then worked for two great companies: McKinsey & Company and General Electric. This training instilled in Hogan the disciplines of strategic thinking and driving results through effective execution.

At Pentair, Hogan was charged with the organizational imperative of building a high-performance company with a heart, although he acknowledged that he hadn't yet connected with the "heart" part of the mission. In the aftermath of firing an executive for unethical conduct, however, he realized that his epiphany of "winning right" was intimately associated with the organization's heart-centered mission.

This new articulation resonated with Hogan in a way that the original wording hadn't, evoking a reconfiguration of the discipline he had learned at his previous companies to embrace a new element—a heart. Thorny issues like decentralization could then be discussed in a different context, which led to a reexamination of other corporate and cultural practices. In essence, Hogan's epiphany sparked a new keystone habit—one that tends to expand and proliferate in many directions—that paved the way for a more adaptive corporate culture and a higher level of organizational discipline.

It's important to note that Hogan's metamorphosis did not require him to disavow his old habits. Instead he layered in patterns from his new mental map, built on "winning right," which created nuanced differences in his leadership. He softened slightly to embrace a new human quality, which aligned with both his own values and those of his company.

Hogan's example shows a new pattern of behavior emerging—new conversations and a new set of routines—along with a new set of rewards that come with better individual and organizational performance.

Now it's your turn to explore your own habits.

Reflective Exercise: Your Adaptive New Habits

Think for a moment about your habits. Hopefully, by reading this book you have become more conscious of all your habits—both the ones that are serving you well and those that are not. This is a good time to flip back in your notebook to review the exercise you did in chapter 3, when you listed your adaptive behaviors and interfering behaviors.

Now think about how your behaviors have changed since you started reading this book. What positive behaviors are you adopting or consciously exhibiting more often? What unproductive behaviors are you abandoning or practicing less often? Are you happy with the changes you've made so far? Are you noticing a difference in how you feel about yourself, your relationships, and your future? Are you receiving any positive feedback from others?

Now let's add two additional considerations. First think about the concept of keystone habits—habits that proliferate in many ways. Part of the power of Hogan's "winning right" philosophy was that it led to new patterns of thought and behavior far beyond the scope of remedying the problem of unethical behavior. Do any of the new habits you're forming have the potential of producing the same leveraging effect?

If you draw a blank here, it may be comforting to know that Hogan himself was surprised at the pervasive effect that "winning right" would have. So don't worry if you don't yet see any keystone habits in your portfolio. Then again, don't underestimate the possibility that one of your new habits may set off a chain reaction of other good habits.

Now let's throw one more consideration into the mix: How do your new or adjusted habits relate to the personal vision statement you crafted in chapter 9? The more dots you can connect between your habits and your vision, the better the chances that you will influence the creation of integrated practices in your organization.

Now that you've thought more deeply about jettisoning old habits and replacing them with new, more adaptive ones, it's time to get more specific and do just that. Ask yourself: *What are the old behaviors I need to stop? What new behaviors do I need to start? What obstacles might crop up as I start adopting these new behaviors?* Write down the answers in your notebook along with a few thoughts about how you intend to overcome those obstacles.

Keep in mind that any change you make in yourself has a ripple effect. Would you notice the difference if everyone you work with became more positive and cheerful? And wouldn't you be more likely to feel positive and cheerful as a result? Like Randy Hogan, whose transformation was grounded in personal practices within an organizational context, you too can have an impact on your organization's culture and behavior. Look at how you answered the questions in the previous paragraph and reflect on the impact that those personal changes could have on the organization as a whole.

Your first reaction might be that, unlike Hogan, you have no control over your organization's practices and behavior. Don't be so sure. Your growth and personal transformation can have a powerful effect on the people around you and the environment in which you work. Your actions, large or small, can be the first step in guiding an organization from where it is now to where it needs to go. As history has shown through the example of Rosa Parks, the African-American civil rights activist who refused to give up her seat on a racially segregated bus, one person's actions can be the catalyst and the inspiration to transform an entire society.

Celebrate What's Precious

Last year my wife's uncle passed away. At the funeral the rabbi praised him for being a mensch—a good person who had lived a life of integrity and honor. The rabbi called his life "precious."

I was struck by his use of that word, and it seemed to heighten my awareness of what is precious in my own life. I started noticing and appreciating things I may have previously rushed past or taken for granted. Each time I slow down and acknowledge something that's precious to me, I feel a sense of elation and contentment, whether it's taking pride in my daughter's accomplishments, sharing a meal with friends, or writing this book.

If you look for precious moments, they are not hard to find. At one of my mindfulness classes, the instructor led our group in a meditation on forgiveness; it was deigned to help us heal our emotional wounds through forgiving ourselves and others. After the meditation, which lasted about 20 minutes, we were given some time to process our feelings. When it was time to end the class and leave, the entire group continued to sit in silence, each of us deep in our own thoughts and emotions yet simultaneously bonded together as a community. We sat for another four or five minutes, and then slowly picked up our yoga mats, put on our shoes, and left. At the next class, we talked about how the experience of dwelling in forgiveness lingered with us, even after we had left the building, and how we carried that experience with us into other encounters and interactions.

As you race through your life, pursuing your goals and ambitions, you may find it transformative, as I did, to continually remind yourself to slow down—to breathe, to notice, to celebrate what is precious.

Of all the leaders I met during my interviews, no one exudes the type of gratitude and appreciation for life's precious moments more than Chuck Denny. Denny has endured more than his share of struggles and heartache. His wife suffered through tuberculosis and breast cancer before ultimately losing her battle with Alzheimer's. They lost three children at very young ages. Yet Denny continues to persist in seeing the bright side of life. Now in his eighties, he told me, "Use your smiles now because you can't take them with you when you die."

Denny humbly credits much of his positive outlook to optimistic genes, but I think there's something else at work. As Denny shared with me his many experiences, first as an executive with Honeywell and then as CEO of ADC Telecommunications, I couldn't help but notice his gift for making others feel genuinely cared for and appreciated by celebrating the goodness in everything they do.

My conversation with Denny reminded me of one of my early teachers, Mr. Levanthal, a kind and gentle soul who taught an after-school class on religion. During winter afternoons we could see the sun go down from our classroom; every time there was a magnificent sunset, Mr. Levanthal would stop the class so that we could admire its beauty. He taught me to celebrate the preciousness of a sunset, a tradition I still practice and pass along to my friends and family.

What is it that you appreciate? What is it that you count as a blessing or a miracle in your life? What are those special moments with family and friends or colleagues that are etched in your mind and maybe even on your soul that nourish you each time you recall them? Perhaps one is as simple as being treated with kindness and compassion by a colleague or stranger. Or maybe it is gratitude for the skills and the talents you bring to your work. Maybe it is simply just being happy, content, and at peace. Do you have a habit of pausing to express your appreciation? What might happen if you make gratitude, appreciation, and celebration a habit or practice personally and in your organization?

Several years ago I had the privilege to serve as my religious congregation's president, where I worked closely with our senior rabbi, Norman Cohen. Rabbi Cohen always tried to bring out the best in me, encouraging me to be the best leader I could possibly become. He told me of a beautiful teaching by the eighteenth-century Hasidic rabbi Zusya. Paraphrasing it for me, he said:

> At the end of your life, God will not ask you why you were not more like Moses. God will ask you why you were not more like Steven.

Throughout this book we've met some very special leaders, but at the end of the day it is best to not judge ourselves by how our own life measures up to that of any of these individuals. Instead a more useful yardstick is how well we find our unique path, tapping into our potential, becoming the best person we can possibly be. The art of struggle lies not in achievements but in the ripples from the journey and how we've grown along the way—the lives we've touched, the kindness we've shown, the ways we've brought to life our most important values. It is the accumulation of all of life's choices, big and small, that creates our unique and personal gift to the world—the world we will bestow on our children.

Additional Resources

$\mathcal{P}$LEASE GO TO THE SNYDER LEADERSHIP GROUP WEBSITE, WWW .snyderleadership.com, for materials that augment and enhance this book. There you will find:

- A computer-based assessment tool to help you construct and navigate through your tension map, hone adaptive energy, and discover potential blind spots; use the code *book2013* to receive a special offer for readers of *Leadership and the Art of Struggle*

- Guided meditations that can be used in conjunction with the exercises of this book

- A leadership notebook, available for purchase, where you can jot down your thoughts as you contemplate the exercises in this book as well as reflect on your leadership journey over the coming months and years

Notes

Introduction

Leadership through a Different Lens

Joe Badaracco's Harvard Business School course examined leadership through the lens of literature. See course syllabus: http://hbsp.harvard.edu/he-main/ resources/documents/web-files/ML_Syllabus_Fall_2001.pdf (accessed September 27, 2012). Joe published many of his ideas from the course in Joseph L. Badaracco Jr., *Questions of Character: Illuminating the Heart of Leadership through Literature* (Boston: Harvard Business School Press, 2006), but the 23-word Struggle Lens was not included in this work, and at the time of this writing has never before been published. I learned about Joe's work through his presentation at the Harvard Business School class reunion in October 2003. He graciously gave his permission to use his formulation as the foundation for my research.

The Art of Struggle: Mastery Practices

I conducted the research for this book while I was an Executive in Residence at the University of Minnesota's Center for Integrative Leadership (2009 to 2010) and an Executive Fellow in Leadership at the University of St. Thomas, Opus College of Business (2010 to 2012). My work draws on 151 examples of leadership struggle from 93 leaders. Data came from two sources: papers written for a class assignment by 58 executive MBA candidates in an organizational behavior class and 90-minute in-depth interviews.

To recruit candidates for the interviews, I relied on a nomination process. I asked people in my network to nominate others whose leadership they admired.

From nearly 100 nominations, I recruited 35 participants, targeting diversity across a number of dimensions, including age, gender, cultural and ethnic background, and industry/sector. The resulting group was 57 percent male and 43 percent female, with ages ranging from 35 to 80 (median age of 56), representing the following populations: CEOs and former CEOs of public companies (20 percent), senior leaders of public companies (31 percent), CEOs/COOs of smaller private companies (26 percent), leaders of nonprofit organizations (17 percent), and leaders from government and the military (6 percent).

In addition to the primary research, this book builds on numerous works of psychological and leadership research. The main theoretic underpinnings of my work are drawn from the following sources: Bill George, *True North: Discover Your Authentic Leadership* (San Francisco: Jossey-Bass, 2007); Warren G. Bennis and Robert J. Thomas, *Geeks and Geezers: How Era, Values, and Defining Moments Shape Leaders* (Boston: Harvard Business Review Press, 2002); Robert J. Thomas, *Crucibles of Leadership: How to Learn from Experience to Become a Great Leader* (Boston: Harvard Business School Press, 2008); Ronald A. Heifetz, *Leadership without Easy Answers* (Cambridge: Harvard University Press, 1998); Morgan W. McCall, Michael M. Lombardo, and Ann M. Morrison, *The Lessons of Experience: How Successful Executives Develop on the Job* (New York: Free Press, 1988); Carol S. Dweck, *Mindset: The New Psychology of Success* (New York: Random House, 2006); and Daniel Kahneman, *Thinking, Fast and Slow* (New York: Farrar, Straus, and Giroux, 2011). These works are cited in detail in various chapters, but overall recognition at the outset is appropriate.

Chapter 1: Struggle Is Not a Four-Letter Word

Rita Marshall is a fictitious name.

The Paradox of the Positive

The positive psychology movement got its official start when Martin E. P. Seligman became president of the American Psychological Association in 1998. In his presidential address, Seligman advocated a shift in psychological research away from single-minded attention to mental illness toward a focus on improving normal life through the study of positive emotions and well-being. Seligman's first book on positive psychology, *Learned Optimism: How to Change Your Mind and Your Life* (New York: Free Press, 1990), as well as Mihaly Csikszentmihalyi's

Flow: The Psychology of Optimal Experience (New York: Harper & Row, 1990), is widely cited. Seligman looked back on his journey in a recent book, *Flourish: A Visionary New Understanding of Happiness and Well-Being* (New York: Free Press, 2011), in which he summarizes some of the key research over the past several decades and provides an expanded and comprehensive description of the underpinnings of positive psychology.

For arguments against positive psychology, see Barbara Ehrenreich, *Bright-Sided: How the Relentless Promotion of Positive Thinking Has Undermined America* (New York: Metropolitan Books, 2009); and Robert B. Kaiser, ed., *The Perils of Accentuating the Positive* (Tulsa: Hogan Press, 2009).

For a balanced analysis of the advantages and the problems of positive psychology, see Beth Azar, "Positive Psychology Advances, with Growing Pains," *Monitor on Psychology* 42 (2011): 32.

Resolving the Paradox

For an in-depth look at the Cuban Missile Crisis, see: Robert F. Kennedy, *Thirteen Days: A Memoir of the Cuban Missile Crisis* (New York: W. W. Norton, 1969).

Two Stories of Struggle

The Anne Mulcahy story was drawn from the following public sources: Bill George, *True North: Discover Your Authentic Leadership* (San Francisco: Jossey-Bass, 2007), 170–74; and Bill George, "America's Best Leaders: Anne Mulcahy, Xerox CEO," *US News and World Report,* November 19, 2008, http://www.usnews.com/news/best-leaders/articles/2008/11/19/americas-best-leaders-anne-mulcahy-xerox-ceo (accessed September 28, 2012).

The Bill Gates material is based on my own experience and recollections. When I was at Microsoft, we referred to the development tools business as the "language business" because, at the time, our business was composed of the programming languages: Assembler, BASIC, C, COBOL, Fortran, and Pascal.

A Lifelong Journey

Gail Sheehy, *New Passages: Mapping Your Life across Time* (New York: Ballantine Books, 1996).

Rita Marshall's essay was published in the *St. Paul Pioneer Press,* November 20, 2011, p. E13, http://www.minnmoms.com/ci_19498940?source=most_viewed (accessed September 28, 2012).

Chapter 2: Adaptive Energy

The concept of adaptive energy is drawn from works by Warren G. Bennis and Robert J. Thomas, *Geeks and Geezers: How Era, Values, and Defining Moments Shape Leaders* (Boston: Harvard Business Review Press, 2002); and Robert J. Thomas, *Crucibles of Leadership: How to Learn from Experience to Become a Great Leader* (Boston: Harvard Business School Press, 2008); and Ronald A. Heifetz's model of adaptive leadership in *Leadership without Easy Answers* (Cambridge: Harvard University Press, 1998).

Adaptive Energy

Mihaly Csikszentmihalyi, *Flow: The Psychology of Optimal Experience* (New York: Harper & Row, 1990).

A Study of Contrasts: Bill Gates and Steve Jobs

The information about Steve Jobs is based on public sources, including Walter Isaacson, *Steve Jobs* (New York: Simon & Schuster, 2011). See quotes on pages 181, 207, 208, and 567.

For the quote from Jobs's August 1997 Macworld Boston speech, see http://www.mac-history.net/apple-history-tv/2008-07-19/macworld-boston -1997-steve-jobs-returns-bill-gates-appeares-on-screen (accessed September 27, 2012).

The Automatic and Reflective Minds

Daniel Kahneman, *Thinking, Fast and Slow* (New York: Farrar, Straus, and Giroux, 2011). Kahneman describes System 1 and System 2 as "agents within the mind." He makes it clear that these do not correspond to actual brain subsystems and goes so far as to call them "fictitious characters." He correctly notes that they are "useful fictions" because they help us visualize and understand how the brain functions. See page 28 for a full explanation. The ball and bat exercise is on page 44. For a very insightful book about the reflective mind, see Kevin Cashman, *The Pause Principle: Step Back to Lead Forward* (San Francisco: Berrett-Koehler, 2012).

Daniel Goleman, *The Brain and Emotional Intelligence: New Insights* (Northampton, MA: More Than Sound, 2011).

Keith E. Stanovich, *What Intelligence Tests Miss: The Psychology of Rational Thought* (New Haven: Yale University Press, 2009), 31.

A description of Steve Jobs's practice of Zen Buddhism can be found on page 35 of the Isaacson biography. For additional information see Joshua Guillar and Karen Neudorf, "Steve Jobs: A Practicing Buddhist, an Entrepreneur, and an Innovator, *Buddhism and Australia*, http://www.buddhismandaustralia .com/index.php/en/articles/40-2012/116-steve-jobs-a-practicing-buddhist -an-entrepreneur-and-an-innovator-joshua-guilar-and-karen-neudorf.html (accessed September 27, 2012).

Chapter 3: Turn Your Energy into Adaptive Energy

Grounding Practice: Adopt a Growth Mind-Set

Carol S. Dweck, *Mindset: The New Psychology of Success* (New York: Random House, 2006).

For more on how the growth mind-set can affect performance, see Robert Wood and Albert Bandura, "Impact of Conceptions of Ability on Self-Regulatory Mechanisms and Complex Decision Making," *Journal of Personality and Social Psychology* 56 (1989): 407–15, http://www.ncbi.nlm.nih.gov/pubmed/2926637 (accessed September 29, 2012).

Grounding Practice: Become Resilient in the Face of Failure

The ABC model was originally created by Albert Ellis, father of Rational Emotive Therapy, in 1962. Here *A* stood for *activating event*. The model was adapted as a foundational element for teaching resilience by Aaron Beck and Marty Seligman at the University of Pennsylvania. An excellent description of the ABC model can be found in Karen Reivich and Andrew Shatté, *The Resilience Factor: Seven Keys to Finding Your Inner Strength and Overcoming Life's Hurdles* (New York: Broadway Books, 2003).

For an excellent book about executive-level resilience, see: Jeffrey Sonnenfeld and Andrew Ward, *Firing Back: How Great Leaders Rebound after Career Disasters* (Boston: Harvard Business School Press, 2007).

Chapter 4: Make Sense of a Chaotic World

Power Struggle

The Joe Dowling story is based largely on my interview. I used the following source to provide additional context of Dowling's tenure at the Abbey: Christopher Fitz-Simon, *The Abbey Theatre: Ireland's National Theatre, The First 100 Years* (London: Thames & Hudson, 2003).

Joseph L. Badaracco Jr., *Defining Moments: When Managers Must Choose between Right and Right* (Boston: Harvard Business School Press, 1997).

James Joyce, *The Portable James Joyce* (New York: Penguin: 1947, 1987), p. 519. (*A Portrait of the Artist as a Young Man* was first published in book form in the United States by B. W. Huebsch, 1916.)

Dowling Epilogue: From "I" to "We"

Bill George, *True North: Discover Your Authentic Leadership* (San Francisco: Jossey-Bass, 2007).

Chapter 5: Regain Balance

The names of Sandy Jones and Lasman's are fictitious.

Grounding Practice: Center Your Mind, Body, and Spirit

Jon Kabat-Zinn, *Wherever You Go, There You Are: Mindfulness Meditation in Everyday Life* (New York: Hyperion, 1994), inside front cover.

For a very vivid account of looking at yourself from the balcony, see: Ronald A. Heifetz and Marty Linsky, *Leadership on the Line: Staying Alive through the Dangers of Leading* (Boston: Harvard Business School Press, 2002), 51.

The stimulus/response quote is from Alex Pattakos, with foreword by Stephen R. Covey, *Prisoners of Our Thoughts: Viktor Frankl's Principles for Discovering Meaning in Life and Work*, 2nd ed. (San Francisco: Berrett-Koehler, 2010), viii. The quote is commonly attributed to Frankl himself, but I traced it to Stephen Covey's foreword. Covey says that he found the quote while wandering through the stacks of a university library in Hawaii. "I did not note the name of the author, so I've never been able to give proper attribution. On a later trip to Hawaii I even went back to find the source and found the library building itself was no longer present."

Kevin Cashman, *Leadership from the Inside Out: Becoming a Leader for Life*, 2nd ed. (San Francisco: Berrett-Koehler, 2008), 149.

Regarding mindfulness and brain function, see Richard J. Davidson with Sharon Begley, *The Emotional Life of Your Brain: How Its Unique Patterns Affect the Way You Think, Feel, and Live—and How You Can Change Them* (New York: Hudson Street Press, 2012), 204.

Regarding the mind/body connection, see Richard J. Davidson, Jon Kabat-Zinn, Jessica Schumacher, et al., "Alterations in Brain and Immune Function Produced by Mindfulness Meditation," *Psychosomatic Medicine* 65 (2003): 564–70.

For the US Army study, see Amishi P. Jha, Elizabeth A. Stanley, Anastasia Kiyonaga, Ling Wong, and Lois Gelfand, "Examining the Protective Effects of Mindfulness Training on Working Memory Capacity and Affective Experience," *Emotion* 10 (2010): 54–64.

Charles Duhigg, *The Power of Habit: Why We Do What We Do in Life and Business* (New York: Random House, 2012).

Grounding Practice: Find the Support You Need

Bill George and Doug Baker, *True North Groups: A Powerful Path to Personal and Leadership Development* (San Francisco: Berrett-Koehler, 2011).

Chapter 6: Navigate Tensions

Navigating through Tensions of Tradition and Aspiration

Target's value of "fast, fun, and friendly" as articulated on the corporate website, http://sites.target.com/site/en/company/page.jsp?contentId=WCMP04-031452 (accessed September 30, 2012).

The quote about Target's value of "speed is life" was taken from the corporate website on August 10, 2011. The site has since been updated and the statement abbreviated. I have included the original quote because it provides a fuller elaboration of this corporate value.

Exploring Practice: Reimagine the Situation to Discover a New Creative Path

The time management matrix is from Stephen R. Covey, *The Seven Habits of Highly Effective People: Powerful Lessons in Personal Change* (New York: Simon & Schuster, 1989).

Chapter 7: Illuminate Blind Spots

Experience Blind Spots: Success Is a Lousy Teacher

Bill Gates, *The Road Ahead* (New York: Viking Press, 1995).

Roger MacMillan is a fictitious name and the details of the situation have been changed, but the overall integrity of the story has been preserved.

Daniel Kahneman and Gary Klein, "Conditions for Intuitive Expertise: A Failure to Disagree," *American Psychologist* 64 (2009): 515–26.

Personality Blind Spots: The Ghost behind the Strength

Jeffrey Sugerman, Mark Scullard, and Emma Wilhelm, *The Eight Dimensions of Leadership: DiSC Strategies for Becoming a Better Leader* (San Francisco: Berrett-Koehler, 2010).

"Report of the Audit Committee of the Board of Directors of Best Buy" to the Board of Directors of Best Buy regarding investigation of alleged misconduct by former chief executive officer, filed in Best Buys' 8-K, May 12, 2012, http://www.bloomberg.com/article/2012-05-14/aMQwdbBDvvTE.html (accessed September 27, 2012).

Values Blind Spots

Freeh Sporkin & Sullivan, "Report of the Special Investigative Counsel Regarding the Actions of the Pennsylvania State University Related to the Child Sexual Abuse Committed by Gerald A. Sandusky, http://www.nytimes.com/interactive/2012/07/12/sports/ncaafootball/13pennstate-document.html (accessed September 27, 2012).

Max H. Bazerman, *Blind Spots: Why We Fail to Do What's Right and What to Do About It* (Princeton: Princeton University Press, 2011).

Strategic Blind Spots

Max II. Bazerman and Michael D. Watkins, *Predictable Surprises: The Disasters You Should Have Seen Coming and How to Prevent Them* (Boston: Harvard Business School Press, 2004).

Conflict Blind Spots

Kathleen A. Kennedy and Emily Pronin, "When Disagreement Gets Ugly: Perceptions of Bias and the Escalation of Conflict," *Personality and Social Psychology Bulletin* 34 (2008): 833–48.

Chapter 8: Transcend Conflict

Stent Wars

The Mike Berman story is based largely on my interview with him, although I also used material from the following sources: Boston Scientific Corporation

8-K filing of April 5, 2001; Barnaby J. Feder, "Boston Scientific Settles with Ex-Partner," *New York Times,* September 22, 2005; Uriel Heilman, "Blood Feud," *Jerusalem Post,* January 12, 2005; and Todd D. Rakoff, "The Case of the Medical Stent," Harvard Law School case study, 2010. The story is told in detail from the Medinol perspective in Guy Rolnik, "When Opportunity Strikes," *Haaretz,* July 22, 2011, http://www.haaretz.com/weekend/week-s-end/when-opportunity -strikes-1.374667 (accessed September 27, 2012).

Transcending Conflict through Compassion and Healing

The names Julie Summers and Tulipville are fictitious.

Chapter 9: Discover Purpose and Meaning through Struggle

For an excellent book on how to find purpose and meaning in your life, see Richard J. Leider, *The Power of Purpose: Find Meaning, Live Longer, Better,* 2nd ed. (San Francisco: Berrett-Koehler, 2010).

Dick Schulze

The *Minneapolis Star Tribune* has extensive coverage on Dick Schulze and Best Buy. To get started see Lee Schafer, "For Schulze, This Is a Most Personal Pursuit," *Minneapolis Star Tribune,* August 20, 2012, http://www.startribune.com/ business/166838186.html?page=1&c=y (accessed September 27, 2012).

Exploring Practice: Recommit, Pivot, or Leap

For more on the concept of pivot, see Reid Hoffman and Ben Casnocha, *The Start-Up of You: Adapt to the Future, Invest in Yourself, and Transform Your Career* (New York: Crown Business, 2012); and Jason Del Ray, "The Art of the Pivot," *Inc.,* February 1, 2011, http://www.inc.com/magazine/20110201/the-art-of -the-pivot.html (accessed September 27, 2012).

Chapter 10: Peer into the Future

For more on Richard Feynman's fascination with the photon and the lifeguard example, see James Gleick, *Genius: The Life and Science of Richard Feynman* (New York: Vintage, 1992).

Steve Jobs, Stanford University Commencement Address, June 2005, http:// www.youtube.com/watch?v=UF8uR6Z6KLc (accessed September 27, 2012).

Deepening Practice: Prepare for What Lies Ahead

For more on the connection between mindfulness and emotional intelligence, see Chade-Meng Tan, *Search Inside Yourself: The Unexpected Path to Achieving Success, Happiness (and World Peace)* (New York: Harper Collins, 2012).

For research about fiction and the brain, see Annie Murphy Paul, "Your Brain on Fiction," *New York Times*, March 17, 2012; Raymond A. Mar, Keith Oatley, Jacob Hirsh, Jennifer dela Paz, Jordan B. Peterson, "Bookworms versus Nerds: Exposure to Fiction versus Nonfiction, Divergent Associations with Social Ability, and the Simulation of Fictional Social Worlds," *Journal of Research in Personality* 40 (2006): 694–712; Raymond A. Mar, Keith Oatley, and Jordan B. Peterson, "Exploring the Link between Reading Fiction and Empathy: Ruling Out Individual Differences and Examining Outcomes," *Communications* 34 (2009): 407–28; and Raymond A. Mar, "The Neural Bases of Social Cognition and Story Comprehension," *Annual Review of Psychology* 62 (2011): 103–34.

For literature as an aid to the development of moral reasoning, see Joseph L. Badaracco Jr., *Questions of Character: Illuminating the Heart of Leadership through Literature* (Boston: Harvard Business School Press, 2006). Also see columns in the *New York Times* by David Brooks, who writes frequently about this issue, for example: David Brooks, "The Service Patch," *New York Times,* May 24, 2012, http://www.nytimes.com/2012/05/25/opinion/brooks-the-service-patch .html (accessed September 27, 2012); and David Brooks, "The Freedom Agenda," *New York Times,* September 20, 2010, http://www.nytimes.com/2010/09/21/ opinion/21brooks.html (accessed September 27, 2012).

Chapter 11: Savor the Marathon

Deepening Practice: Harness the Engine of Discipline

Charles Duhigg, *The Power of Habit: Why We Do What We Do in Life and Business* (New York: Random House, 2012).

Deepening Practice: Celebrate What's Precious

The Rabbi Zusya story is from Martin Burber, *Tales of the Hasidim: The Early Masters* (New York; Schocken Books, 1947).

Acknowledgments

$\mathcal{A}$N AUTHOR'S FIRST BOOK TENDS TO BE A JOURNEY THROUGH THE wilderness. My heartfelt gratitude goes to those who have steered me through the thickets of uncertainty, provided me with encouragement, and pointed me toward the open clearings of awareness and discovery.

I start with my wife, best friend, and soul mate, Sherry Stern, to whom this book is dedicated. Your unbounded love and patience have meant the world to me over the 40-plus years we've known each other and the 34 years of our marriage. Thank you for always believing in me, especially during those times when I didn't believe in myself.

To Elana, our daughter, you inspire me and fill my heart with joy as I watch you grow into the beautiful young woman you are. I am proud of your every accomplishment but even prouder of the person you've become.

To my mom, Florence Snyder, and my dad, Harold Snyder of blessed memory, who lovingly guided me during my formative years. To my brother, Mark Snyder; my sister-in-law, Lenni; and my nieces, Sarah and Hannah, from whom I've learned so much.

To Bill George, I am grateful for your mentorship and friendship. You seemed to know exactly the right words that would guide me through this project at every step along the way. Thank you for writing the foreword and for helping me find and express my True North through this book. To Joe Badaracco, special thanks for entrusting your insightful leadership lens to my custody and for your helpful feedback and guidance.

I am especially grateful for the work of two incredibly talented developmental editors—Margie Adler and Phil Bolsta—with whom I worked at different stages of the project. Each of you in your own way added your brilliant insights, the genius of your craft, and your relentless passion and drive for excellence. Thanks also to Karin Odell for her creative design of the illustrations.

I am deeply grateful to Todd Sattersten, my book coach, whose BizBookLab inspired me and taught me the foundations of book authorship. And to Neal Maillet, my editor at Berrett-Koehler, who believed in this project from the start and patiently taught me how to transform my rough ideas into a publishable book.

I am also indebted to Neal for bringing me into the Berrett-Koehler family. It is truly a blessing and a privilege to be part of such an inspiring and generous community. Special thanks to community organizer in chief Steve Piersanti, as well as other members of the Berrett-Koehler community who helped produce this book and bring it to market: Maria Jesus Aguilo, Marina Cook, Michael Crowley, Kristen Frantz, Zoe Mackey, David Marshall, Gary Palmatier, Dianne Platner, Courtney Schonfeld, Cynthia Shannon, Jeevan Sivasubramaniam, Elizabeth von Radics, Rick Wilson, and Ian Shimokviak, who designed the book cover. A special shout-out and word of appreciation to my fellow BK authors for their friendship and mentorship: Steve Arneson, Wendy Axelrod, Ken Blanchard, Dianna Boher, Noah Blumenthal, Kevin Cashman, BJ Gallagher, Laura Goodrich, Vicki Halsey, Jennifer Kahnweiler, Bev Kaye, Richard Leider, Barbara McAfee, Mark Miller, Craig and Patricia Neal, Dennis and Michelle Reina, Mike Song, Jesse Lyn Stoner, Bill Treasurer, and Leslie Yerkes.

To the reviewers who reviewed a preliminary draft of this book, thank you for your insightful feedback: Kathy Flanagan, Sara Jane Hope, David Schmaltz, and Jim Wylde.

I am indebted to my friends at the University of St. Thomas, who welcomed me with open arms, provided me with generous financial support, and created a nurturing climate for me to do my research. Special thanks to Dean Chris Puto as well as Sandy Beach, Dawn Elm, Michael Garrison, Ken Goodpaster, Pat Hedberg, Ron James, Dave Jamieson, Doug Jondle, Dean Maines, Jack Militello, Christopher Michaelson, Michael Porter, David Rodbourne, Teresa Rothausen-Vange, Kate Schaefers, Brian Shapiro, Bob Shoemake, and Ertugrul Tuzcu.

I also appreciate the help of my friends at the University of Minnesota—at the Center for Integrative Leadership, Center for Spirituality and Healing, Carlson School of Management, Psychology Department, and Creative Writing Department. Special thanks to Laura Bloomberg, Joyce Bono, Trish Hampl, Mariann Johnson, Mary Jo Kreitzer; Dianne Lev, Myles Shaver, Mimi Sprengnether, Auke Tellegen, Paul Vaaler, and my former business ethics students at the Carlson School.

Thank you to the great leaders who participated in my research for generously and openly sharing your stories: David Abelson, Marc Belton, Duane Benson, Mike Berman, Mary Brainerd, Armando Camacho, Chuck Denny, Joe Dowling, Dave Durenberger, Andy Grossman, Esperanza Guerrero-Anderson, Kate Herzog, Randy Hogan, Deb Hopp, Joe Kelly, Marci Malzahn, Ken Melrose, Kevin Rhein, Frank Russomanno, Dick Schulze, Mark Sheffert, Danielle Steinberg, Kathee Tesija, Bob Wahlstedt, and Joellyn Veninga as well as all of you who, for various reasons, remain anonymous.

A special word of gratitude and appreciation to my friends and colleagues from various walks of life, who have shared their ideas and in one way or another assisted me with this project: E. Abraham, SJ; David Abrams; Monica Abrams; Nisha Advani; Cino Adelson; Calvin Allan; Erin Albert; Sharon Arad; Brett Atkin; Nadine Babu; Doug Baker; Ralph Bernstein; Greg Bell; Brenda Boehler; John and Fauzia Burke; Angie Butcher; Marilyn Carlson Nelson; Steve Carples; John Chisholm; Paul Cimmerer; Rabbi Norman Cohen; Deb Cundy; Mike Davis; Brian Davis; Tricia Dirks; Yale Dolginow; Shelly Dolley; Carol Donen; Karen Failes-Coad; Chuck Feltz; Joe

Folkman; Doreen Frankel; Dee Gaeddert; Liz Garrett; Larry Getlin; Michael Gorman; Cliff Greene; Terri Griffith; Stephanie Grossman; Stan Halle; George Hallenbeck; Jim Hansen; Barbara Henricks; Andy Herring; Rick Hilman; Katherine Holt; Jim Hornthal; Ralph Jacobson; Sam Joseph; Hubert Joly; Cindy Johnson; Joyce Juster; Michael and Shelly Kassen; Kelly Kingman; Rob Kieval; Gene Kim; Jodee Kozlak; Jim Kouzes; Angie Lalor; Mark Levy; Brad Lehrman; Eric Levinson; Rabbi David Locketz; David Magy; Gil Mann; Tracy Maurer; Karen May; Dick McNeil; Carolyn Monaco; Daina Middleton; Paul Mooty; Gary Musyznski; Frederick Nemer; Kaila Nickel; Kevin Nilan; Debra Orenstein; Cara Peck; John Pershing; Karen Poel; Karen Preston; Dave Pylipow; Kamala and Prakash Puram; Lou Quast; Trudy Rautio; Diane Rawlings; John Riedl; Sandy and Earl Reiland; John Roberts; Becky Robinson; Bob Romasco; Maurrie Salenger; Susan Savkov; Rusty Shelton; Nathan Shore; Marc Sokol; Mary Schmidt; Darcy Stivland; Jeff Sugerman; Ricky Surie; Peter Vrijsen; Wendy Wade; Ann Winblad; Marsh Walzer; Irv and Marge Weiser; Bob Whitman; Kevin Wilde; Emma Wilhelm; Susan Williams; and Michael Young.

To all of my friends at the various organizations I've been associated with over these many years, either as an employee, a volunteer, or a student: University of Pennsylvania, Boston Consulting Group, Touche Ross & Co, Microsoft, Hennepin County Medical Center, Personnel Decisions International, Net Perceptions, Bet Shalom Congregation, Minneapolis Jewish Federation, Hillel at the University of Minnesota, Minneapolis Jewish Community Foundation, Masterman Junior High School and Central High School in Philadelphia, Drexel University, Harvard Business School, University of Washington, and University of Minnesota. You are wise colleagues and teachers and I most humbly appreciate your gifts, which have had a lasting effect on me.

Finally, special thanks to you, my readers, who have patiently stayed with me until the very end. May your struggles reveal their gifts to you, and may you use them wisely.

Index

About the Author

STEVEN SNYDER, PhD, IS THE FOUNDER OF Twin Cities–based Snyder Leadership Group, an organizational consulting firm dedicated to cultivating inspired leadership. Snyder has developed the breakthrough concepts introduced in *Leadership and the Art of Struggle* based on years of research, including extensive interviews with senior executives from major corporations as well as his personal experience working closely with Bill Gates.

Snyder joined Microsoft in 1983, when that company was in its infancy. His work there, praised by Gates, secured the relationship with IBM during a crucial stage in Microsoft's growth and helped shape the history of the personal computer industry. Promoted as Microsoft's first business unit general manager, Snyder led the company's development tools business, where his team won *PC Magazine*'s prestigious Technical Excellence Award on three occasions.

After his influential tenure at Microsoft, Snyder earned a master's degree and a doctorate in psychology from the University of Minnesota. He applied his multidisciplinary background to initiate innovative software for human resource development at Personnel Decisions International, a worldwide human resources consulting firm.

When Internet advancements drew Snyder's attention, he joined forces with computer scientists from the University of Minnesota to pioneer a groundbreaking technology called collaborative filtering. As co-founder and CEO of Net Perceptions, he successfully commercialized this invention to enable the real-time personalized recommendations that have become central to the online experience. This groundbreaking work won Snyder the first-ever World Technology Award for Commerce for "contributing to the advance of emerging technologies for the benefit of business and society."

In addition to his work with Snyder Leadership Group, Snyder was an Executive in Residence at the University of Minnesota's Center for Integrative Leadership and is currently an Executive Fellow in Leadership at the University of St. Thomas Opus College of Business. Snyder also taught business ethics at the University of Minnesota's Carlson School of Management for seven years.

Snyder has been a guest on ABC-TV's *Nightline* as well as a featured speaker in North America, Europe, and Asia. He was selected to deliver the seventeenth JRD Tata Oration on Business Ethics in Jamshedpur, India.

In addition to his psychology degrees, Snyder earned a bachelor's degree in mathematics from Drexel University and a master's degree in business administration from the Harvard Business School, where he was a Baker Scholar. He currently lives with his family in the Minneapolis area, where he remains actively engaged in philanthropy and community service.

Here's how you can connect with Steven Snyder:

Twitter: @Steven_J_Snyder

LinkedIn: www.linkedin.com/in/stevensnyder

Facebook: www.facebook.com/artofstruggle

Website: www.snyderleadership.com

Berrett–Koehler
Publishers

Berrett-Koehler is an independent publisher dedicated to an ambitious mission: Connecting people and ideas to create a world that works for all.

We believe that the solutions to the world's problems will come from all of us, working at all levels: in our organizations, in our society, and in our own lives. Our BK Business books help people make their organizations more humane, democratic, diverse, and effective (we don't think there's any contradiction there). Our BK Currents books offer pathways to creating a more just, equitable, and sustainable society. Our BK Life books help people create positive change in their lives and align their personal practices with their aspirations for a better world.

All of our books are designed to bring people seeking positive change together around the ideas that empower them to see and shape the world in a new way.

And we strive to practice what we preach. At the core of our approach is Stewardship, a deep sense of responsibility to administer the company for the benefit of all of our stakeholder groups including authors, customers, employees, investors, service providers, and the communities and environment around us. Everything we do is built around this and our other key values of quality, partnership, inclusion, and sustainability.

This is why we are both a B-Corporation and a California Benefit Corporation—a certification and a for-profit legal status that require us to adhere to the highest standards for corporate, social, and environmental performance.

We are grateful to our readers, authors, and other friends of the company who consider themselves to be part of the BK Community. We hope that you, too, will join us in our mission.

A BK Business Book

We hope you enjoy this BK Business book. BK Business books pioneer new leadership and management practices and socially responsible approaches to business. They are designed to provide you with groundbreaking and practical tools to transform your work and organizations while upholding the triple bottom line of people, planet, and profits. High-five!

To find out more, visit **www.bkconnection.com.**

Berrett–Koehler
Publishers

Connecting people and ideas
to create a world that works for all

Dear Reader,

Thank you for picking up this book and joining our worldwide community of Berrett-Koehler readers. We share ideas that bring positive change into people's lives, organizations, and society.

To welcome you, we'd like to offer you a free e-book. You can pick from among twelve of our bestselling books by entering the promotional code **BKP92E** here: http://www.bkconnection.com/welcome.

When you claim your free e-book, we'll also send you a copy of our e-newsletter, the *BK Communiqué*. Although you're free to unsubscribe, there are many benefits to sticking around. In every issue of our newsletter you'll find

- A free e-book
- Tips from famous authors
- Discounts on spotlight titles
- Hilarious insider publishing news
- A chance to win a prize for answering a riddle

Best of all, our readers tell us, "Your newsletter is the only one I actually read." So claim your gift today, and please stay in touch!

Sincerely,

Charlotte Ashlock
Steward of the BK Website

Questions? Comments? Contact me at bkcommunity@bkpub.com.

MIX
Paper from
responsible sources
FSC
www.fsc.org   **FSC® C016245**

Certified

Corporation
bcorporation.net